THE SONS OF SAM

SEAMUS MALONEY works for the *Irish News* in Belfast. While he inherited a love of Gaelic football from his Donegal father, hurling is his real sporting passion and he follows his native Antrim with the eternal hope that this year could be their year. He also plays, when selected, for the Latharna Óg club in Larne. This is his first book.

THE SONS OF SAM

Ulster's Gaelic Football Greats

Seamus Maloney

THE BREHON PRESS
BELFAST

First published 2004 by The Brehon Press Ltd

1A Bryson Street, Belfast BT5 4ES, Northern Ireland

ISBN 0 9544867 4 9

Design: December Publications

Printed in Ireland by Betaprint

CONTENTS

Dedicated to the memory of Kathleen Maloney

ACKNOWLEDGEMENTS

First of all, thanks must go to the McAnallen family for allowing me to use material gathered in an interview with Cormac a little over a month before his death.

No player I approached to interview hesitated in giving me their time and sharing their memories. Thank you Mick Higgins, Paddy Doherty, Ross Carr, Noel Hegarty, Enda Gormley, Brendan Tierney and Cormac McAnallen.

The thought of writing a book would never have entered my head had it not been for Brendan Anderson and Damian Keenan, my publishers at the Brehon Press. I was already aware that Brendan was a great teacher; now I also know he is great to work for. Damian showed amazing trust in letting someone barely two years at the job loose on a book and great patience when he had to wade through it.

At the *Irish News*, thanks are due to editor Noel Doran and librarian Kathleen Bell. My colleagues in the sports department deserve many thanks for encouragement, advice, proof reading, suggestions, phone numbers, switching shifts – the lot really. Cheers to Thomas Hawkins, Kenny Archer, Kevin Farrell, Michael McWilliams, Paddy Heaney, Brendan Crossan, Paul McConville, Barry Delargy, John O'Connor, Eamonn O'Hara and Thomas Hawkins jnr. My gratitude is extended to Ann McManus, Hugh Russell, Brendan Murphy, Niall Carson and Seamus Loughran from the picture desk for allowing me to use their excellent photographs.

That I have any interest at all in Gaelic football is down to having a father who grew up in a house on the mouth of Teelin Bay in south-west Donegal. Chapter seven, which is inspired by the magical summer we shared following Donegal to Croke Park in 1992, is dedicated to Jimmy Maloney.

Others who helped get this book written, maybe without realising it, include Eugene Markey and Savina Donohoe at the Cavan County Museum in Ballyjamesduff, John McEvoy and the staff of the Crannog Bookshop in Cavan, Mickey Harte, Kieran McDaid, Barney Cully, Eamon Gaffney at the *Anglo-Celt*, Matt Fitzpatrick, Kevin Boyle, Paddy Graham, Eoin McQuillan, Chris Gilbert, Gay and George Glynn, Geraldine and Peter Rooney, Ambrose Kennedy, Ray McManus at *Sportsfile*, the staff at the National Library of Ireland in Dublin, and my brother Brian Maloney.

Finally, my thanks go most of all to Jennifer: for everything.

PICTURE CREDITS

All photographs and illustrative material is reproduced by kind permission of the following: Cavan County Museum, pages 12-59 and first colour section pages 1-3; the *Irish News* (Ann McManus, Hugh Russell, Brendan Murphy, Niall Carson and Seamus Loughran), pages 96-208, first colour section pages 4-7, bottom picture on page 8, and all pictures in second colour section; the *Irish News* archive pages 63-64, 67 and 76; Oliver McVeigh, first colour section, top picture on page 8; Gerry Quinn, page 60; Sean Magee, page 71; and Peter Rooney, pages 72, 81, 86, 90, 91 and 93. Every reasonable effort has been made to contact the copyright holders of photographs reproduced in the book. If any involuntary infringement of copyright has occurred, sincere apologies are offered and the owners of such copyright are requested to contact the publishers.

INTRODUCTION

'Observe the Sons of Ulster Marching Towards the Sam.'

The headline in the *Sunday Tribune* on 28 September 2003 said it all. The allusion to the title of the Frank McGuinness stage play about the horrors of the First World War had first been used four weeks earlier in GAA president Sean Kelly's programme notes for the All-Ireland semi-final between Donegal and Armagh. It had also featured atop countless newspaper stories since.

The final was in a sense Ulster football's finest hour. It prompted the biggest cross-border exodus since Pope John Paul II's visit to Ireland in 1979 and, for a day, made Dublin look like a small market town in Monaghan.

The 'back door' system introduced in 2001 had made it possible that two teams from the same province could contest the All-Ireland title. In 2003 this possibility became a reality as early as mid-August when Tyrone beat Kerry in the first semi-final. The meeting between Donegal and Armagh a week later was, from an Ulster point of view, merely dotting the *'i's* and crossing the *'t's*.

While Ulster enjoyed a warm glow of satisfaction, much of the rest of the country grumbled that the northern teams were ruining football and had turned it into a battle of strength rather than skill. Armagh and Tyrone didn't pay a blind bit of notice and just got on with it.

This attitude has marked Ulster football since the start of the GAA. The provincial championship in the north has always existed as a separate entity from the rest of the country, and although the 'back door' has opened up the championship, there remains something aloof about the games played in Casement Park, Breffni Park and Clones each summer.

The Ulster championship is arguably the most competitive provincial championship, and for years this was to the detriment of Ulster's All-Ireland hopes. From Down's All-Ireland win in 1968 to Tyrone's in 2003, only three counties retained their provincial title: Derry in 1975-76, Tyrone in 1995-96 and Armagh in 1999-2000. Counties played in Croke Park one year, sometimes well, sometimes not; sometimes even won, but couldn't build on their experience because their championship ended in Omagh or Ballybofey the following year. Even when Down, Donegal and Derry put together an unprecedented run of success in the early 1990s, none of these teams successfully defended their Ulster title.

The 'back door' brought second chances, more games at Croke Park and, though traditionalists will lynch you for saying so, more opportunity for the best team to rise to the top.

Since Offaly won their first All-Ireland title in 1971, just four other counties have added their names to the Sam Maguire, all of them from Ulster: Donegal, Derry, Armagh and Tyrone. Each win was celebrated with more fervour than the last. No one enjoys a meal more than a hungry man.

The level of All-Ireland celebration in Ulster counties isn't just because winning the Sam is a novelty. Gaelic games in the north, particularly in Northern Ireland, are approached differently than in the rest of the country. Political considerations mean that belonging to a GAA club in Newbridge, County Derry is different to belonging to a club in Newbridge, County Kildare. When being a GAA member could cost you your life, as it did many times in Northern Ireland's troubled past, watching your county win the ultimate prize – or helping them win it – means much more.

This book touches on that aspect of the GAA in Ulster, but it isn't about it. It isn't really about the GAA in Ulster either; it's about the fourteen teams from the northern nine counties that have won the All-Ireland senior championship. It doesn't pretend to examine the development of GAA clubs, or the many disappointing losses that Ulster counties, including Antrim, Fermanagh and Monaghan, suffered on the provincial or national stage.

Each county, each year or glory, each near miss, could command a book on its own. This particular book is quite narrow in focus, but Ulster's achievements can expand it. They already have.

When the idea of this book first came up, Armagh were the reigning All-Ireland champions, and the story would have stopped there. By the time the book was underway, Tyrone had forced their way into the pages. By the time you read this, the book may already be out of date. As a proud follower of Ulster GAA, I sincerely hope it is.

1

'Second To None'

CAVAN 1933, 1935

Cavan, the first county to bring Sam north, the county with the most Ulster senior titles and more All-Ireland final appearances than any other Ulster county, was not even in the GAA for two months in 1930.

A wrangle with the Ulster council over the venue of that year's provincial final meant that, for forty-seven days between 10 August and 27 September, the Cavan county board was not affiliated to the GAA. This came just two years after Cavan's initial All-Ireland appearance when Kildare beat them by a point to become the first county to lift the new Sam Maguire Cup.

1929 hadn't gone so well for Cavan. The Ulster final against Monaghan at Breffni Park finished 1-4 apiece and the replay in Carrickmacross went in Monaghan's favour, 1-10 to 1-7. The visitors were angry about the condition of the pitch, claiming it was too small, and complained of verbal abuse from the crowd, especially towards their star player Jim Smith.

The same two counties qualified for the 1930 final and the Ulster council voted to hold the game at Carrickmacross. Cavan were unhappy and said they were prepared to play anywhere but the Monaghan ground. They asked for a change of venue and warned the council that a Carrickmacross final might result in no Cavan team playing on the day. The council rejected Cavan's appeal and the Cavan board decided not to travel.

Council secretary B.C. Fay, a Cavan man, claimed the county board's decision wasn't the view of Cavan gaels. A team was put together and did travel, but it wasn't close to full strength and lost 4-3 to 1-5.

A flurry of exchanges followed, with the Cavan board condemning those who had organised the team to go to Carrickmacross. The Ulster council, in turn, declared that the meeting at which the decision was made not to travel had not been properly constituted.

At that same meeting the provincial council was also faced with notification that Cavan would not travel to face Donegal in the junior championship at Ballyshannon on 10 August. Failure to field would see the whole county suspended for twelve months. On 11 August the Ulster council met to enact Rule 13, under which they were able to take over GAA matters in the county. A split seemed inevitable, but a compromise was eventually reached, with both sides admitting some culpability in the whole messy affair. A special convention on 27 September under GAA president Sean Ryan readmitted Cavan and the episode was eventually put to bed.

Two years later Cavan were All-Ireland champions.

 As was common in the early days of the GAA, the 1911 All-Ireland final wasn't played in 1911; instead, it took place on 14 January 1912. This delay meant that Antrim, the first Ulster county to feature in a final, attained the dubious distinction of being the only county to lose two All-Ireland senior football finals in the same year. First the Shaun's club from Belfast was well beaten by Cork representatives Lees by 6-6 to 1-2 in the January match; then the Mitchel's club was defeated on 3 November 1912 by Louth champions Tredagh.

In 1928 Cavan made the first of their ten appearances in the All-Ireland senior final when, after winning their twenty-eighth Ulster title, they beat Sligo in the semi-final to qualify for a meeting with reigning champions Kildare. A controversial goal from Kildare full-forward Paddy Loughlin helped the holders retain their title 2-6 to 2-5 and captain Bill Gannon became the first man to be presented with the Sam Maguire Cup.

In 1930, a day after a special convention readmitted Cavan to the GAA following the 'Carrickmacross affair', Monaghan were soundly beaten 3-11 to

In 1928, the first Cavan team to contest an All-Ireland final lost by a point to Kildare. The Sam Maguire Cup was on offer for the first time that year.

0-2 by Kerry in the Ulster county's only final appearance.

The trauma caused by the threatened split of 1930 wasn't allowed to affect Cavan's progress and, in 1931, the county reached its first National League final. However, they couldn't claim the title and Kerry won by a point, 1-3 to 1-2. Ulster titles followed in 1931 and 1932, but Cavan failed at the All-Ireland semi-final stage each year: first to Kildare, then Mayo. Both years, Kerry beat Cavan's semi-final conquerors and, with their 1932 win over Mayo, the Kerry men equalled Wexford's record of four All-Ireland titles in a row.

Cavan had a bye through to the semi-finals of the 1933 Ulster championship, due to the non-participation that year of Derry and Donegal, so filled the time with challenge matches. They drew with Mayo in Castlebar in a repeat of the previous year's All-Ireland semi-final, then played host to the Connacht champions in Breffni Park a week later. While no cups would be won or lost, the *Anglo-Celt* was sure of the game's importance.

'No contest since the famous match with Kildare at Breffni Park two years ago has aroused such widespread interest – it is looked upon as a real championship affair – and the attendance should mark a record for a game of its class.'

A big crowd did show up and saw the home side produce an impressive 2-12 to 1-5 win. Cavan's next outing was the real thing – an Ulster semi-final against Armagh, a repeat of the 1932 provincial final. The win over Mayo had convinced the *Anglo-Celt* there wouldn't be an upset.

'The games with Mayo were impressive, and their big score in the last demonstrated accurate forward work which should pull them through on Sunday.'

When Sunday came, Cavan failed to turn on the style as they had done against Mayo and recorded an unremarkable, workmanlike 1-8 to 0-2 win. Armagh had faded after a bright start, but even then Cavan failed to rack up the total their possession demanded. The *Anglo-Celt* wasn't impressed.

'The shooting of each set of forwards was rather faulty, for which there is little excuse with a dry ball and closely shaven dry sod.'

Armagh opened the scoring, but M.J. Magee managed to pull Cavan level. Hughie O'Reilly was at the centre of things for the reigning champions and forced a good save from the Armagh goalkeeper. Jack Smallhorne centred for Louis Blessing to gather, and he fisted the ball to Vincent McGovern for Cavan to take the lead. Their next score effectively ended the contest as Packie Devlin managed to get in a low shot that fizzed past Houlihan to the Armagh net. Armagh were still attacking, but couldn't find their range from frees or from play and Cavan knocked over two more points before the break.

First Devlin set up McGovern for a point; then Blessing fired over a superb score from near the end-line to give Cavan a 1-4 to 0-1 half-time lead. As in the first half, Armagh opened the scoring, this time with a Frank Toner free, but that proved their last score.

Hughie O'Reilly and Cornafean's Tom O'Reilly were dominating midfield and Cavan continued to keep the scoreboard ticking. Magee kicked over from near the corner, then Tom O'Reilly boomed over a long-range free. Blessing forced a good save from Houlihan, but Devlin managed to collect the rebound and score a point. The game was becoming increasingly scrappy and littered with frees. 'With eight minutes to go, and Armagh fighting a forlorn battle,' reported the *Anglo-Celt*, 'the game lost interest.'

Magee took a pass from Blessing to record the final point and give Cavan a nine-point win and a place in the Ulster final. Tyrone and Fermanagh were set to contest the other semi-final and the *Anglo-Celt* was in no doubt which side would win.

'Fermanagh are hot favourites as finalists and if it works out that they meet Cavan, the final should be one of the greatest of recent years.'

Fermanagh, however, lost 1-4 to 1-3 and Tyrone, in their first provincial final, provided Cavan's opposition.

Before the final Cavan took part in another challenge match, this time against Kildare, to mark the opening of the new Cusack Park in Mullingar. Dublin and Kerry also featured, with Kerry billed as the 'World's Champions' after their recent successful tour of America. An extra treat for the paying customers was that the game would start with the ball being dropped out of an aeroplane: 'an innovation,' said the *Anglo-Celt*, 'which in itself is worth going a big journey to see'. Cavan lost to Kildare 1-6 to 1-4, but all the talk was about the aeroplane.

'There was audible excitement and expectation when the drone of the monoplane was heard. All eyes stared skywards as the silver coloured machine approached and, after performing many "stunts", it came nearer to earth and dropped the ball which fell near the Kildare posts, the players having already taken up their positions all over the pitch. The crowd cheered loudly and play then began.'

Back on firm ground, the *Anglo-Celt* speculated what Tyrone might bring to their first Ulster final appearance.

'We understand that the Tyrone men are undergoing a special course of preparation for the final … It is a healthy sign to find teams getting ready for an important event of the kind and with respect it goes without saying that the Cavan boys are not idle either, as nothing can be left to chance.'

There was no need to be too cautious as Cavan trounced Tyrone 6-13 to 1-2. Cavan were hot favourites going into the match, but Tyrone's case wasn't helped by their county board's decision the Friday before the game to suspend the Dungannon Clarke's club and, with it, five of the senior county team. The *Anglo-Celt* wasn't pleased.

'In view of the proximity of the final, and of its importance as the chief event in the province, it was a mistake that such drastic action was not deferred.

'No domestic trouble should have been permitted to weaken a county team as those who travel to see a final expect to find both sides at full strength. They come to see a good game and it was no wonder to find such

The Cavan team before their All-Ireland final meeting with Galway in 1933

universal disappointment expressed over Sunday's debacle.' Even if the Dungannon players had been available, it was still unlikely that Tyrone would have troubled Cavan. The Ulster final rookies were not impressive.

'Tackling was of a very puny description,' stated the *Anglo-Celt*, 'and their kicks were short and poorly directed. It is just a mystery how they succeeded in getting over Antrim and Fermanagh on their way to the final.'

Tyrone started steadily enough and the opening point of the game didn't come until Jim Smith, the Cavan captain, making his first championship appearance of the season, kicked over a free from forty yards, off the top of the crossbar. Once Cavan got their first score they started to open up. Donal Morgan pointed from close range, then M.J. Magee collected a free from Hughie O'Reilly and kicked over. Cavan's fourth point came in the twelfth minute from Magee. Three minutes later Cavan scored the first of their six goals. Jack Smallhorne dispossessed his marker before firing in a centre that found its way to Magee via Vincent McGovern, and Magee made no mistake.

A second quickly followed from Eamon Briody and two more points gave Cavan a commanding 2-6 to no score lead. Tyrone finally managed a point after twenty minutes. Cavan replied with another goal, this one from McGovern, and Smallhorne and Morgan added two quick points. The agony wasn't over for Tyrone as a Packie Phair free struck the post and fell nicely to Packie Devlin, who goaled. Magee found the net again right on the whistle to give Cavan a 5-8 to 0-1 lead at the break.

Many spectators cut their losses and started to head home, but Cavan kept on scoring, with Devlin, Magee and Briody combining for 1-2, Briody finding the net.

'Monotonous play continued and Devlin, as if for variety, had an overhead point,' was how the *Anglo-Celt* put it.

Devlin added another, then Magee scored again before Tyrone enjoyed a flourish of their own to end the game when, right on the full-time whistle, Ed McGee found the net.

Cavan were back in the All-Ireland semi-final and the county board wasted no time in making sure the players would be well prepared for it, placing advertisements asking for contributions to a training fund:

'Appeal for funds for the training of the Cavan County Team to play Munster at the All-Ireland semi-final on the 27th August. Subscriptions are currently solicited from all those desiring to ensure that Ulster's prestige is upheld. Any amount will be gratefully accepted.'

Earlier in the summer, central council had voted to stage the semi-final between the Ulster and Munster champions at Breffni Park. Therefore, the meeting with Kerry, 'World Champions', and going for an unprecedented fifth All-Ireland title in a row, generated more interest than usual in Cavan and Ulster. The *Anglo-Celt* stated that:

'Of all the big matches in which Cavan has taken part there is none to compare, on point of feverish anticipation, with that of Sunday next when they meet the redoubtable Kerry men at Breffni Park in the semi-final of the All-Ireland championship.'

As well as stirring up interest in the game, the newspaper was forthright in handing out advice to the Cavan team.

'It is well the players should remember that their supporters expect them to go "all out" from the throw-in, instead of playing a "waiting game" for the first quarter of an hour.

'It is also important that the Cavan team should not overlook the value of the point. The men in the scoring line should seize every opportunity to pile up points. On former occasions opportunities were lost in futile efforts to find the net, while valuable points were thrown away. Let it not be so on this occasion.

'A parting word of advice to them – when the ball is thrown in on Sunday … get to their work without delay. That delays are dangerous is an old axiom, and pertains especially to football … Now or never!'

On 27 August 1933, Cavan's moment was now. An official attendance of 17,111 – the biggest crowd ever at an Ulster football match – watched Cavan dramatically end Kerry's hopes of five in a row. Six days later the *Anglo-Celt* started its report:

'Although the smoke of battle has more or less disappeared and things returned to normal, it is still difficult to describe in cold print the wonderful achievement of the Cavan team – an event of worldwide importance – in defeating the famous Kerry men, Irish champions for four years in succession, by one goal five points to five points in the All-Ireland semi-final at Breffni Park on Sunday last.'

Cavan captain Jim Smith (right) and Galway skipper Mick Donnellan lead their teams on the pre-match parade before the 1933 All-Ireland final

Perhaps the paper can be forgiven for losing the run of itself a little. The 'international' incident started at a frenetic pace. Jackie Ryan got the first score from a twenty-five-yard free and doubled Kerry's advantage after seventeen minutes. Cavan had opportunities, but couldn't find the target, while they were riding their luck in defence, requiring assistance from the woodwork twice. Magee finally got them off the mark with a short-range free after twenty-five minutes. A heavy shower before the match had made the surface very slippery and both sides were having problems keeping their footing and getting accurate shots in. At half-time Kerry led 0-2 to 0-1.

Micko Doyle pointed a 'fifty' to stretch the Kerry lead at the start of the second half, and from the kick-out, Paul Russell kicked over to extend that lead 0-4 to 0-1. Packie Phair found M.J. Magee with a free with ten minutes left and Magee pointed from a narrow angle to cut the gap to two. It was down to one when Dan O'Keeffe tipped over Donal Morgan's shot, but Kerry extended their advantage again when Ryan pointed. Cavan replied through Jack Smallhorne, then Magee equalised with a thirty yard free. The crowd could sense something special might happen. As the *Anglo-Celt* put it:

'The memories of the disappointments of nearly half a century seemed to imbibe the Cavan men with determination not to let victory slip from their grasp.'

With two minutes left Cornafean's Tom O'Reilly launched another attack that finished with Vincent McGovern fisting to the net to give Cavan a three-point lead. The crowd went mad, but it was nothing compared to their reaction at the final whistle.

'The scene which follows baffles description. Hats, coats, umbrellas and many other articles were thrown skywards, and the people were wild in their enthusiasm.

'Hoary headed men who have followed the fortitudes of the team unflinchingly for 40 years shouted exaultingly, and one was heard to exclaim, "Thank God I lived to see the day."'

Coverage of the result wasn't confined to the sports pages and the *Anglo-Celt* editorial roundly praised Cavan's achievement which, it said, was about more than football.

'The moral which the game conveys might well be taken to heart by many others than Gaels as it shows that whatever we are engaged at, and no matter how formidable the opposition might be, the fight should be carried on with grim determination, as it is often at the very last moment that the reward comes, after an honest and sustained struggle.'

The win wasn't just for Cavan either. The victory, 'while a magnificent testimony to the victors' play, should give encouragement to the Gaels of the whole of Ulster, and to those of all other counties in Ireland as well'.

The prevailing mood in Cavan was that the Kerry game had been the real All-Ireland final and Galway would pose little difficulty in the decider itself. The Cavan team and management left nothing to chance. They retired, as they had done before the semi-final, for a month's training to the Greenville Hotel in Belturbet.

'We know that the Cavan men are in good hands and that no stone will be left unturned to bring the Blue Ribbon to Breffni and Ulster,' boasted the *Anglo-Celt*. 'A senior final between Connacht and Ulster is unheard of in Gaelic annals. Truly we are making history.'

1933 wasn't Cavan's first All-Ireland final, but the interest generated by the defeat of Kerry, and the expectation that Galway would fall as well, created a level of excitement comparable to that in a county going through the experience for the first time. Some correspondents were moved to poetry.

We thank the boys who lifted old Breffni from the dark,
And we'll all be there to cheer them to victory in Croke Park.
The young and sere will all be there and it's soon I'll make a start,
As I want to get before them in my good old ass and cart.

Advertisements for special trains to the game, as well as restaurants and hotels in Dublin, filled the papers. The county board took out another notice asking for money for the training fund:

'The magnificent victory of our County Team has cheered the hearts of Cavan and Ulster men the world over. For their loyal support we are deeply grateful. With confidence we appeal to our supporters for the necessary financial assistance to enable the team to win for Cavan and Ulster the First Senior All-Ireland Final.'

Galway's rearguard feels the pressure against Cavan

Cavan people made their way to Dublin by every means possible. Eight hundred were on the train from Killeshandra alone, while cars and open lorries carried others who got soaked along the way when the heavens opened. Every vehicle from Swanlinbar was in Dublin, while others cycled to the capital from as far away as the Fermanagh border. When they got there, Cavan supporters set the standard for Ulster fans heading to Croke Park in the years to come. According to the *Irish Independent*:

'Nothing like the display of colours, blue and white, sported by the Cavan supporters has been witnessed on the streets of the capital on the occasion of an All-Ireland final before … Just before the match one would think that half the population of Ulster had been emptied onto the streets.'

Five of the Cavan team had appeared in the 1928 final: Willie Young, Patsy Lynch, Hughie O'Reilly, Packie Devlin, and captain Jim Smith. Smith won the toss and elected to play with the breeze in the first half, but Galway opened the scoring after two minutes. Cavan were back on terms five minutes later when M.J. Magee's free hit the top of the crossbar and bounced over. Heavy rain before the match had made the surface difficult and both sets of players had trouble keeping their feet.

Another Magee free put Cavan a point up, but Galway equalised immediately, Mick Higgins collecting from Brendan Nestor and kicking over. Three minutes later Jim Smith lined up a free from forty yards, which flew straight past Galway goalkeeper Michael Brennan into the net. Cavan were

The great Cavan full-back Patsy Lynch moves to clear his lines

buoyed by the score and kept up the tempo, and Packie Devlin kicked them five points ahead after twenty-seven minutes. Cavan followers would have been happy enough with that margin at the break, but just before the whistle Magee sent a high lob towards the Galway posts. This was collected by Louis Blessing, who transferred back to the in-rushing Magee, who fisted to the net. Cavan were well on their way to the title, leading 2-3 to 0-1 at half-time.

The rain fell heavier as the second half got underway and Galway quickly hauled themselves back into contention when Nestor shot to the net after a scramble in the Cavan goalmouth three minutes after the restart.

Mick Donnellan forced a good save from Willie Young, but the resulting 'fifty' from Higgins found Donnellan again, and he kicked Galway's second point. Galway voices in the crowd, quiet for much of the game, picked up, but they were silenced again when Jack Smallhorne collected from Devlin and kicked over another point.

With twelve minutes left Nestor converted an easy free, but it proved Galway's final score. As the final whistle neared, Cavan full-back Patsy Lynch and Donnellan collided, leaving Lynch prone on the ground. Lynch had to be taken to the Mater Hospital and, as he left the field, both sets of players knelt together to pray for his recovery. The *Anglo-Celt* described Cavan's final point:

'In the last minute Devlin got hold about 30 yards out, roved to the open, took a glance for the posts and blarged the ball, striking the right post as it fell over for the final point of the game.'

When the final whistle confirmed Cavan's 2-5 to 1-4 win, the county's joyous followers engulfed the pitch and chaired their captain Jim Smith to the Hogan Stand, where he became the first Ulsterman to lift the Sam Maguire. Smith was delighted.

'My life's ambition is now realised,' he said, 'for after 14 years of struggle I have what I want at last.'

The first Ulster team to lift Sam was:

CAVAN 1933
Willie Young

Willie Connolly	Patsy Lynch	Mickey Dinneny
Terry Coyle	Jim Smith	Packie Phair
Hughie O'Reilly		Tom O'Reilly (Cornafean)
Donal Morgan	Packie Devlin	Jack Smallhorne
Vincie McGovern	Louis Blessing	M.J. 'Sonny' Magee

Substitutes
Tom Crowe, Paddy McNamee, Paddy Brady,
Tom O'Reilly (Mullahoran), Jack Rahill

Cavan, All-Ireland champions in 1933

That night, the victorious party were guests at a banquet in the Shelbourne Hotel, hosted by Cavan residents in Dublin. The journey north was illuminated by numerous bonfires and, when they finally made it back to Cavan on Monday evening, the town was packed with people to welcome them home. Writing in the *Anglo-Celt*, 'J.F.' summed up the feeling of a whole county:

'On Sunday Jimmy Smith and his men "brought home the bacon", so I will put on the kettle and make tea and may you all be as happy as I feel today.'

1933 closed on a losing note when, with the ring of All-Ireland celebrations still in the air, Meath ended Cavan's double hopes by beating them in the National League final.

The next year, the golden jubilee of the GAA, Cavan enjoyed a tour of America as All-Ireland champions. They arrived in New York on 14 May and played their first game in front of 40,000 people against the home side at Yankee Stadium. It finished in a draw, 1-7 each. The team went on to Philadelphia, Boston, New Jersey and then back to New York before heading home to defend their Ulster and All-Ireland titles.

Ulster was easily annexed with a simple 3-8 to 0-2 final victory over Armagh. The All-Ireland semi-final against Galway was set for Parkmore in Tuam, but it soon became clear that the venue couldn't handle the 25,000 spectators that showed up. Pitch 'invasions', which were in fact spillage of the crowd onto the field because people had nowhere else to go, meant that the first half lasted forty-eight minutes. From start to finish the game took two

The Cavan team on their way back from their successful tour of America

hours to complete. The Connacht champions held on for a 1-8 to 0-8 victory, and although Cavan appealed to the central council, it fell on deaf ears and their All-Ireland title was gone.

The 1935 Ulster campaign opened with a trip to Bundoran to face Donegal. Although the *Anglo-Celt* cautioned that the hosts were 'a dashing, heavy team that will take some beating', Cavan weren't expected to have any problems. In the end they were lucky to make it out of the seaside town with a 1-11 to 1-9 win.

Cornafean's Tom O'Reilly opened the scoring in the first minute and the Cavan lead was doubled when M.J. Magee pointed a 'fifty'. Magee was on target again when he took a pass from Packie Devlin to record Cavan's third point.

Brian Winston got Donegal off the mark with a free, but Magee replied in kind before the home side registered their second point. For the next fifteen minutes Cavan laid siege to the Donegal goal. Magee and Paddy McNamee kicked points and Hughie O'Reilly bundled in a rebound after Devlin's fierce shot had been saved. Pat Boylan joined the fun with a point, then had a goal disallowed before Jack Rahill tapped over for another Cavan score.

Donegal got over their shock and managed the next three points, but Jack Smallhorne completed the first half scoring to put Cavan 1-9 to 0-5 up at the break.

Two points from Hugh Gallagher opened the second half for Donegal and Magee managed one for Cavan. A Brady point and a Doyle free cut the margin to four, then Gallagher scrambled in a goal to leave just one between the sides. The crowd urged Donegal upfield, but they couldn't find the equaliser. Boylan got the last score and Cavan were glad to escape with a narrow win.

Cavan went into their Ulster semi-final clash with Monaghan a week after losing the McKenna Cup final to their neighbours, 2-7 to 1-7, but completed as complete a turnaround as is imaginable, winning the championship game 2-12 to 0-1. It was a baffling scoreline.

'The difference was so marked that one could scarcely believe it was practically the same 15 which beat Cavan by a goal that day week in the Dr McKenna Cup final,' pondered the *Anglo-Celt*. 'This all goes to show the glorious uncertainty of football, and what may happen in a week or a day, but it is not easy to explain away the lengthy margin.'

Four minutes into the game M.J. Magee hit Cavan's first point from out on the wing, and he added another before Monaghan got their first score. Cornafean's Tom O'Reilly won the kick-out and got the ball to Paddy McNamee, whose cross was punched to the net by Louis Blessing. Packie Devlin helped himself to three points, while Magee added another. Devlin found the net just before the break to leave Cavan leading 2-5 to 0-1 at half-time. Monaghan were shell-shocked, but things got worse with the restart. Devlin opened Cavan's second half account and more scores followed as

Monaghan, totally dispirited, simply played out time.

After the surprising goings-on of the Monaghan game, the Ulster final against Fermanagh was eagerly anticipated.

'Not for years past has an Ulster senior final been looked forward to with such interest and enthusiasm as that which takes place at Belturbet on Sunday week between Cavan and Fermanagh,' the *Anglo-Celt* enthused. 'It is bound to be the stiffest contest in recent years and should rank as the most thrilling in the annals of Ulster Gaeldom.'

It didn't, and Cavan eventually won 2-6 to 2-1 in a match 'more remarkable for its robustness than brilliance'. The most interesting moments of the afternoon came when referee Tom Shevlin received a few errant Cavan passes in the first half due to his partly blue attire. Some drama also arose when two unfortunate members of the press, on finding that their seats had been taken, were forced to watch the game while sitting on an upturned orange box which didn't bear their weight for long.

On the field, Cavan shot out of the blocks and M.J. Magee tapped in a rebound after two minutes. Jack Smallhorne won the kick-out and pointed from thirty yards before adding another long-range point in the fifth minute. Hughie O'Reilly got a point, then a high ball dropped into the Fermanagh square and, as the defence tried to clear, Louis Blessing and Paddy McNamee bundled defenders and ball into the net for a goal.

Fermanagh replied with a goal of their own when a long drive from Jim McCullagh found Billy Maguire unmarked inside, and Maguire thumped home from twenty yards. McCullagh wasted an opportunity to bring Fermanagh to within a point when he blasted a penalty wide, but the Ernemen did find the net again two minutes after half-time.

Cavan picked up the pace again with two unanswered points and, although Maguire raised a white flag for Fermanagh, Hughie O'Reilly, the best player on the pitch, completed the scoring.

Tipperary provided the opposition in the All-Ireland semi-final, but much of the talk in Cavan leading up to the game concerned the availability of Jim Smith. Smith was a spectator at a match featuring a garda team in Dublin and got involved in a disagreement with the referee. He was suspended by the Dublin county board and, when he didn't appear at a hearing into the case, it seemed the suspension would rule him out of the 'Tipp' game. In the end it took a special meeting of the county board in Croke Park an hour before the game was due to start to clear him to play. The general feeling in Cavan was that their All-Ireland experience would show itself on the big day.

'Most of them have proved their worth in the past and also in the recent provincial championship,' stated the *Anglo-Celt*, 'and there is every reason for confidence in their ability to beat Tipperary, or any other county, for that matter.'

They did beat Tipperary, but they barely deserved it. In the end it took a goal in the dying seconds to see off the Munster champions 1-7 to 0-8. It was, according to the *Anglo-Celt*, a thrilling finish.

Cavan take to the pitch before their 1935 All-Ireland final clash with the 'lily-whites' of Kildare

'Perhaps one of the most sensational finishes in connection with an All-Ireland Championship was staged in the last moments of the Semi-Final between Cavan and Tipperary on Sunday … Tipperary players were flabbergasted and their backers dumbfounded.'

Walter Scott opened the scoring for Tipperary in the second minute, but M.J. Magee cancelled out the score four minutes later. Cavan started to move

Cavan goalkeeper Willie Young under pressure from the Kildare attack

well, particularly in the forwards, and points followed from Devlin and Magee, who kicked one from play and one free.

Thomas O'Keeffe got one back for Tipperary, but Magee was back on target with two more to give Cavan a 0-6 to 0-2 lead. Tipperary rallied as half-time approached and Kieran Holland sandwiched a Richard Power point with two frees to leave just a point between the teams at the break.

Holland levelled ten minutes into the second half and Dick Allen gave Tipp a deserved lead when he volleyed over the bar. Holland kicked a long-range point and Cavan were in serious trouble. A Magee free from out on the left cut the deficit to one; then, in added time, Jim Smith aimed a 'fifty' for the posts and Hughie O'Reilly fisted it to the net. Tipperary claimed time was up when the goal went in and also lodged an objection over the eligibility of Smith. Both protests failed and Cavan were back in the All-Ireland final.

Cavan were underdogs for the final clash with Kildare, who had been impressive in their semi-final win over Mayo. Despite this, the editorial page of the *Anglo-Celt* was sure Cavan could do the job.

'Full of admiration for the gallant Kildare, we wish them a good display, but we are confident, as are the Breffni representatives, that this year's crown shall come once again to the North.'

Pat Boylan fists the ball towards the Kildare goal

Cavan's Pat Boylan scores his, and his county's, second goal in the 1935 final

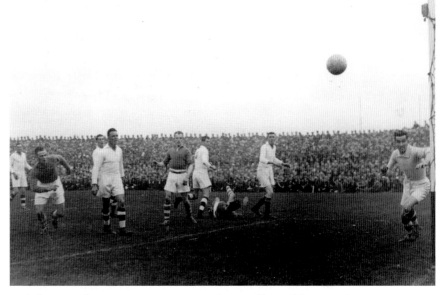

The squad was again training at Greenville and letters of encouragement poured into the camp:

'Dear Smith,
'Sir, a few lines I hope to convey to you the battle you and your men have before you. Cavan can win if they like. All they have to do is keep cool, keep even in the first half. In the second half fight all the way. Kildare say that you never beat them yet. They beat you on your own ground in Breffni Park. Think of it. They say you have no sting. How will you beat them in Croke Park? If you take control in the second half you will win by a decisive victory. At all costs win. Don't lose your heads but don't be like a lot of old women. Fight for victory and victory is yours. If you don't win I'll shoot the whole lot of you.
Signed – County Down.'

The correspondent from the Mournes had no need to load his gun. In front of a 50,380-strong crowd Cavan destroyed Kildare.

Louis Blessing scored the first point within a minute and, although Michael Geraghty equalised four minutes later, Cavan went on a 1-4 scoring run. Two points from M.J. Magee and one each from Jack Smallhorne and Hughie O'Reilly were added to by a goal from Pat Boylan.

Thomas Mulhall managed to pull a goal back for Kildare, but Boylan replied with his second of the day soon after. Paddy Martin got the last point of the half for Kildare, but the 'lily-whites' were still 2-5 to 1-2 down at the break.

Five minutes into the second half Mullahoran's Tom O'Reilly effectively ended the game with Cavan's third goal, and Packie Devlin added a point a minute later. Kildare completed the scoring with an unanswered 1-2,

Mickey Dinneny (number 4) looks on as his colleagues in the Cavan full-back line try to keep the Kildare forwards at bay

Geraghty finding the net with sixteen minutes left, but Cavan held on for a famous 3-5 to 2-4 win.

Once again their supporters celebrated; once again Dublin played host to a northern invasion.

'In moving through the city streets and at the grounds, one was struck by the ring of sharp Northern accents and it can be safely assumed that three fourths of the attendance was from the North.'

It was Hughie O'Reilly's turn to bring the Sam Maguire north and the *Anglo-Celt* couldn't resist basking in the glory.

'The Cavan victory may not be popular in some quarters but they are champions again in spite of all that, and had justice been meted out to them in connection with the game at Tuam they would now probably be holders of the Blue Ribbon for three years in succession, which is more than other pretentious counties can boast of.'

Cavan's winning fifteen were:

CAVAN 1935

Willie Young

Willie Connolly · Jim Smith · Mickey Dinneny

Terry Dolan · Tom O'Reilly (Cornafean) · Packie Phair

Hughie O'Reilly · Tom O'Reilly (Mullahoran)

Donal Morgan · Packie Devlin · Jack Smallhorne

Pat Boylan · Louis Blessing · M.J. 'Sonny' Magee

Substitutes
Tom Crowe, Paddy McNamee, Paddy Brady, Tom O'Reilly, Jack Rahill

For the second time in three years a jubilant crowd welcomed the Sam Maguire back to Cavan town. Jim Smith addressed the crowd from the platform.

'I think we have placed Cavan on the map,' he said, 'and that we proved yesterday beyond reasonable doubt that Cavan is one of the greatest Gaelic counties in Ireland.'

The crowd cheered and a voice was heard to shout: 'Second to none.'

Hughie O'Reilly

Man of the Match: Hughie O'Reilly

Nobody has played such a major role in more Ulster All-Ireland successes than Hughie O'Reilly. The Cornafean man was midfield in the Cavan team that brought Sam to Ulster for the first time and captained them from the same position to their second title two years later. He also played in Cavan's inaugural, and unsuccessful, All-Ireland final appearance in 1928.

His midfield partnerships – first with 'Big' Tom O'Reilly from Cornafean, then Tom O'Reilly from Mullahoran – were crucial to Cavan's domination of Ulster and their two Sam Maguire victories in the 1930s.

He eventually hung up his boots in 1941, but remained involved with the county senior team when he assumed the role of trainer. From the sidelines he achieved even more success and helped maintain Cavan's position as the pre-eminent force in Ulster football. Outside the province, O'Reilly's training was a key factor in bringing Cavan three more All-Ireland titles in 1947, 1948 and 1952, as well as a National League win in 1948.

As a trainer, he insisted on mastery of the same skills that had marked him out as an exceptional footballer: the basics of catching, kicking and passing. His experience on the field meant he was a respected figure among the players and he always seemed to get the maximum amount from the teams with which he was involved. In his pursuit of the best, he came up with a list of 'tips' for playing the game.

1. Play your own area
2. Goalie: keep backs in position
3. Full-backs: clear ball to wings
4. Backs: mark closely, but at the same time dominate play
5. Backs: keep between opponent and goal
6. Half-backs: place forward with clearance
7. Backs: meet incoming forwards
8. Always mark free kicks
9. Never let the ball hop
10. Never turn your back on ball
11. Two kicks are greater than one
12. Get in front of opponent
13. When not in possession, get into position
14. Keep up pressure
15. Don't hesitate to shoot inside thirty yards
16. Shoot for points, goals will follow
17. Move into position for pass
18. Full-forwards: remember half-forwards
19. Play ball on ground
20. Go forward to meet the ball
21. Kick ball before being tackled
22. Always play the ball
23. Avoid clashing
24. Keep trying
25. Remember: opponent is getting it as hard as yourself
26. Keep moving all during game and take deep breaths
27. Get off the ground when about to receive a knock
28. Go out and win, but for God's sake, *play the game*

2

'See You in New York'

CAVAN 1947, 1948

The 1947 season was arguably the most significant in the history of American sport.

After decades of segregation and discrimination, Jackie Robinson trotted on to Ebbets Field and became the first black man to play the 'national pastime' of baseball for a major team – the Brooklyn Dodgers. Robinson's outstanding play aided the slow process of breaking down racial barriers, and helped the Dodgers into the World Series that year, which they lost to the New York Yankees.

The Big Apple's other team, the New York Giants, meanwhile, didn't fare so well that year. However, their home – the Polo Grounds – made a bit of history itself when it played host to one of the most important events in Irish sport: the All-Ireland senior football final between Cavan and Kerry.

 The idea of bringing the All-Ireland final across the Atlantic was first mooted by John Kerry O'Donnell of the GAA's New York board, but only gained real momentum when the president of the Munster council, the Very Reverend Canon M. Hamilton of Clare, got behind it. A proposal was made at the Clare convention in January 1947 to move the final Stateside, and was passed at the annual congress on Easter Sunday later that year.

One of the reasons for the move was the fact that 1947 marked the centenary of the Great Famine and, as such, presented an ideal opportunity to make a gesture towards America's Irish emigrant population. Additionally, the GAA saw benefits for itself since the Second World War had, among other things, ended the touring of county teams to the States, and a New York final would be a chance to strengthen the Association's Trans-Atlantic links.

The news of an American All-Ireland final was greeted with some excitement by county players, such as Cavan's Mick Higgins.

GAELIC ATHLETIC ASSOCIATION
FOUNDED 1884

OFFICIAL SOUVENIR PROGRAMME
ALL IRELAND FOOTBALL CHAMPIONSHIP FINAL
at
POLO GROUNDS, NEW YORK
SEPTEMBER 14th, 1947

SUBSCRIPTION 50c

The one that got away: Joe Stafford gets ready to score a goal in the 1945 All-Ireland final against Cork. Unfortunately, Cavan came up short in the end by four points

The match programme for the 1947 All-Ireland final at the Polo Grounds in New York

'At that time teams didn't go on trips out of the country as much as they do now, so it was something new. Canon Hamilton from Clare had brought up the idea at central council and it was a way of kind of lifting spirits after the war, and raising interest in the GAA in America.

'The decision was made on Easter Sunday and we were actually playing Kerry in London on the Easter Monday when the news came through to us. I remember one of the Kerry players saying: "We'll see you in New York." Little did we think at that stage that he would be right.'

Cavan remained a force on the national stage in the period after 1933 and 1935, but couldn't manage another All-Ireland title. They were deprived of their crown in 1936 when Laois shocked them in the All-Ireland semi-final and they lost a final replay to Kerry the following year. A new generation of players helped them into the 1943 final, but a replay was their undoing again. Two years later Cork beat them by four points in the final.

1945 brought Cavan's seventh Ulster title in a row, but Antrim surprised them in 1946. They went into 1947 eager to get back on top in Ulster, then maybe plan for a trip to America. As it happened, when the championship

came around they nearly didn't get past Monaghan. Mick Higgins, who was a member of the 1943 and 1945 panels, knows how fortunate they were.

'We were very lucky to get a draw with Monaghan in the first game. They played well that day and maybe thought they should have beaten us. John Joe O'Reilly missed the penalty at the end, but still, we very nearly went out.'

Monaghan had the breeze at their backs for the opening thirty minutes and got the first point from a fourteen yard free. Sixty seconds later Mick Higgins replied in kind for Cavan.

Paddy O'Rourke took back the lead for Monaghan before Edwin Carolan recorded Cavan's second equaliser from an acute angle. Carolan's point spurred his team into a bit of life and they kicked over the next three scores through Higgins, John Joe Cassidy and Tony Tighe.

Murphy steadied Monaghan with another short-range free, then the sides swapped the final two points of the half to leave the score 0-6 to 0-4 in Cavan's favour at the break.

Monaghan tore into their neighbours from the restart and quickly registered a goal and a point to go into the lead. With the score-line unexpectedly against them, Cavan rallied and Tighe equalised in the forty-eighth minute. They took back the lead when Higgins pointed, but Monaghan didn't buckle and got their reward when Eugene McDonald equalised. However, there was still time for Cavan to spurn the chance to avoid a replay. In the last minute the Breffni men were awarded a penalty and, instead of tapping over for a point and probable victory, captain John Joe O'Reilly inexplicably went for goal. The shot was saved, Monaghan cleared, and the sides had to meet again.

The replay was equally competitive. The first six points were shared before Peter Donohoe put Cavan in front after Edwin Carolan was fouled. T.P. O'Reilly doubled the lead, but the favourites were let off the hook when Hughie McKearney hit the post. Paddy O'Rourke kicked his third point for Monaghan, but Tony Tighe pushed Cavan two points ahead when he finished a quick break out of defence started by P.J. Duke. Frees from Ollie O'Rourke brought Monaghan level, but Joe Stafford punched an opportunist goal to give Cavan the advantage. Paddy O'Rourke pulled Monaghan a point closer before half-time and they went in trailing 1-6 to 0-7.

Monaghan were within one when a McDonald kick bounced over the bar, but two Donohoe frees re-established the three-point margin.

The lead didn't last long as Monaghan pulled themselves level with a goal ten minutes from the end. That score brought the sides level for the sixth time, but Cavan responded as they had in the drawn game, and reeled off three unanswered points. Monaghan didn't throw in the towel and McKearney forced a spectacular save from Vincent Gannon. Vincent Duffy managed a point, but that was it for Monaghan, and Cavan scraped through 1-11 to 1-9.

It seemed that Tyrone might pose as stern a test as Monaghan when they scored the first two points of the Ulster semi-final in Dungannon, but Cavan quickly took control of the game, accumulating points and goals in the face of little Tyrone resistance. The only other scores of the first half came from two Peter Donohoe frees, the tally kept down by the teeming rain.

Joe Stafford followed Donohoe's second half opener with a goal. Then, seventeen minutes after the break, Columba McDyer provided the ammunition for Edwin Carolan to ripple the net. Three minutes later a forty-yard free from Donohoe travelled straight to the Monaghan net and Simon Deignan hit Cavan's fourth goal before points from John Joe Cassidy and Stafford completed the scoring at 4-5 to 0-2.

After enduring the deluge in Dungannon, another downpour greeted Cavan when they travelled to Clones to face the reigning Antrim in the Ulster final. Mick Higgins felt Antrim weren't helped by the conditions.

'Antrim were our biggest worry at that time. They had a very good team, but they just didn't get it right in that final. It was a terrible wet day, and I think that the weather suited us more than them because they used to do an awful lot of hand-passing. We did some ourselves, but we mainly just kicked on and let the ball do the work.'

Cavan's first half performance was enough to wrest the provincial title away from the champions. They were already a point ahead when T.P. O'Reilly's shot was deflected into the Antrim net by full-back Mal McMahon. Cavan didn't let up and took every chance they got. Joe Stafford pointed; then two goals followed: the first a fourteen-yard free blasted in by Peter Donohoe, the second scored by Stafford who finished a four-man move started by Mick Higgins.

Antrim finally got on the board when Sean Gibson pointed. Kevin Armstrong doubled their tally, but Stafford completed the scoring for the half to give Cavan a 3-3 to 0-2 lead.

Antrim came into the game as the break approached and they picked away at Cavan's lead through the second half. Points from Joe McCallin, Peter O'Hara and a couple of frees had reduced the deficit to six when full-forward Frank Dunlop hammered in a goal with eight minutes left. That was as good as it got for Antrim, and Peter Donohoe tacked on a final point to make Cavan safe at 3-4 to 1-6.

With a trip to New York at stake, the 1947 All-Ireland semi-finals took on a deeper significance. They were also the last chance supporters at home would get to see their counties in action that summer so, unsurprisingly, both games set attendance records.

66,000 people packed Croke Park to see Kerry beat Meath and earn a place against Cavan, who had already booked their spot in the final thanks to a surprise victory over Roscommon in front of 60,000 spectators.

'Roscommon were favourites to beat us in the semi-final,' says Mick Higgins, 'but we played well and deserved it. We were definitely the better team.'

Cavan were out of the blocks quickly and had two Peter Donohoe points on the board before Brian O'Rourke got Roscommon off the mark in the ninth minute. Two Donohoe frees sandwiched a couple of Roscommon

The advance party of substitutes and officials on board the Mauritania en route to New York

points; then the Mountnugent man took a pass from Tony Tighe to blast in a goal. Cavan led 1-4 to 0-3 at the break, thanks entirely to Donohoe.

An O'Rourke free opened the second half scoring, and he added another with forty-two minutes gone after Jack McQuillan was fouled going through. McQuillan had actually put the ball in the net but, to the dismay of the Roscommon players and supporters, the referee called back the play.

Cavan's lead had been pegged back to two, but Tighe restored their cushion by capping a brilliant run with a fierce shot that bounced back onto the field off the goal stanchion. J.J. Nerney got a goal back for Roscommon, but Cavan held on to book their ticket to the States with a 2-4 to 0-6 win.

On Tuesday, 2 September an advance party of twenty-five, including GAA officials, substitutes and officers from both Cavan and Kerry boarded the *Mauritania* at Cobh and set sail for New York. As the boat arrived the following Monday, the remainder of the travelling party began their plane journey. Mick Higgins remembers that it was quite an experience.

'The substitutes and officers went on ahead by boat, then the players went out by plane. It wasn't the best: twenty-nine hours to get there. We arrived down at Rineanna, as Shannon was then, and were held up for four hours, so that was a good start. It's a good thing we were there as a group, because after

Coach Patrick Lynch performs a hand-to-toe with an imaginary ball while James Cassidy, Tom O'Reilly and Eunan Tiernan look on. The picture was taken as the Mauritania *arrived in New York on 8 September 1947*

that, I don't think we would have bothered to go over if we had been going individually.

'We had to go by the Azores because that's where you had to refuel. Then, when we started out again, one of the engines gave up and we had to come down again. It was more nerve-racking than the game. We were long in the air and long on the ground.

'We were in an American army plane and we weren't prepared for the experience. We hit air pockets a few times and they hadn't been explained to us. We thought we were gone once or twice.'

Once they got to America, the Cavan and Kerry players were treated to a ticker tape parade. They were greeted by New York mayor Bill O'Dwyer, who hailed from Mayo, and a crowd of five thousand people. The two teams visited the Polo Grounds on the Friday before the game, but found the pitch rock-hard, the wrong size, half dirt, half grass, and with the baseball mound still intact. It didn't help matters that New York was also in the middle of a heatwave.

'The pitch in the Polo Grounds was very poor,' Mick Higgins recalls. 'It was very hard and not really playable, but once we won we didn't worry too much about that.'

The teams and officials attended a celebration of Mass by Cardinal Francis Spellman in St Patrick's Cathedral on the morning of the game, 14

The Polo Grounds – normally home to baseball's New York Giants – marked out and ready for the Gaelic football invasion

September, before making their way to the ballpark. The crowd was less than expected and the 34,941 attendance didn't trouble the seating arrangements in the cavernous Polo Grounds. The two teams paraded around the field, led by the New York Police Department Band, which played '*Amrhan na bhFiann*', 'Faith of Our Fathers' and 'The Star Spangled Banner'. Mayor O'Dwyer threw in the ball and Kerry got down to business very quickly.

A point from Tom O'Connor and a goal from Batt Garvey had already been earned by the time Peter Donohoe kicked Cavan's first score from a free. O'Connor added 1-1 from the seventh minute to the tenth and, although Columba McDyer managed a point, two more Kerry scores gave the Munster champions an eight-point lead.

The last two Kerry points came after P.J. Duke and Tony Tighe moved to right half-back and midfield respectively, but that switch started to pay dividends as the half wore on. Donohoe chipped over a couple of frees, then Tighe found Joe Stafford who went past corner-back Dinny Lyne and scored a goal.

Duke instigated the six-man move that finished with Mick Higgins scoring Cavan's second goal and transforming a 2-4 to 0-2 score-line against into a 2-5 to 2-4 lead in the twenty-eighth minute. Cavan had the initiative and continued to turn the screw as Kerry wilted in the pitiless heat.

'Kerry started very well and they were leading by eight points after about fifteen minutes,' says Higgins. 'But then we got a grip on the game and got the ball moving. We went in at half-time leading by three points. It was a

The Cavan and Kerry teams and officials on the steps of New York's City Hall ahead of the 1947 All-Ireland final

terrible warm day and the Kerry players were mostly older than we were, so I think the heat maybe affected them more than us, but we were the better team overall. Whether or not the heat had a lot to do with it, I don't know. We came from behind, and it was a good match to come from behind and win. You'd like to do that in an All-Ireland final in Croke Park.'

Donohoe continued to prove his accuracy from frees in the second half and picked off points at regular intervals, finishing with 0-8. Arthur Daly of the *New York Times* awarded him the title of 'the Babe Ruth of Gaelic football'.

Mick Higgins, himself born in New York, finished the scoring and the game concluded 2-11 to 2-7 in Cavan's favour. John Joe O'Reilly accepted the Sam Maguire in the unique setting of the New York Polo Grounds – the home of the Giants.

CAVAN COLORS: BLUE

The Breffni men as shown in the 1947 final programme

Cavan's history-making team was:

CAVAN 1947		
	Vincent Gannon	
Bill Doonan	Brian O'Reilly	Paddy Smith
John Wilson	John Joe O'Reilly	Simon Deignan
P.J. Duke		Phil Brady
Tony Tighe	Mick Higgins	Columba McDyer
Joe Stafford	Peter Donohoe	T.P. O'Reilly

Higgins recalls that the American press reaction to the game was almost unanimous in its praise.

'The Americans were thrilled with it. The match was played at a very fast pace, and they couldn't believe that we were amateurs. Even though it was boiling hot, the tempo kept up and the Americans were amazed that it was non-stop action, instead of the stopping and starting they were used to with their sports.

'There was no negative football in it. The game was played in very good spirit and there were no injuries or knocks. It was the type of game you would have liked to watch yourself.'

After a celebratory dinner for both teams in the Commodore Hotel, both parties headed home together aboard the *Queen Mary* on the Wednesday after the final, arriving in Southampton eight days later. Then it was off to Dun Laoghaire and Dublin, where the players attended receptions at the Mansion House and Arás an Uachtarain. Even so, Mick Higgins believes All-Ireland winners in later years had to go through a lot more rigmarole.

'There was a civic reception in Dublin for us when we got back, but there still wasn't as much excitement and hype as there would be now. There wasn't the same publicity, even though at the time going to America to play a football match was a very big thing.'

It was certainly a big thing in Cavan and fifteen thousand supporters were waiting in the county town to welcome their heroes when they got home on Monday, more than a week after their historic triumph.

 Cavan continued to win into 1948 and qualified for the National League final with a two-point victory over Kerry. They drew with Cork in the final, 2-11 to 3-8, but the replay, which Cavan won 5-9 to 2-8, wasn't held until 24 October. In the meantime, Cavan won the championship again.

Down were first up in Lurgan, and Cavan ran out comfortable 2-9 to 1-4 winners. Peter Donohoe got the ball rolling when he punched home a T.P.

O'Reilly centre to open the scoring. Cavan tacked on six more points from six different players, all from play. Down pulled a goal back, but points from Donohoe and Higgins made sure any revival was short-lived. A couple of points gave Down some hope, but Higgins kicked over two himself before Joe Stafford fed Donohoe, who scored Cavan's second goal. Down rounded off the scoring with Barney Carr getting the last point of the game, but Cavan were not troubled in their passage to an Ulster semi-final meeting with Monaghan.

In that game, Cavan quickly exploited the breeze and were three up in five minutes. Both sides survived early goal scares before McDonald opened Monaghan's account with a free in the seventeenth minute, and he hit another one just before half-time. However, these came in between points from John Joe Cassidy, Higgins, and a couple of Peter Donohoe frees which helped Cavan to a 0-7 to 0-2 half-time lead.

Like Monaghan in the first half, Cavan managed just two scores in the second, but crucially, one was a superb individual goal from Tony Tighe. This boost came after Monaghan had scored the first two points of the half, and gave Cavan a six-point lead. Paddy O'Rourke's final point for Monaghan brought them within five, but Cavan held on for a 1-9 to 0-7 win.

The 1948 final renewed the biggest Ulster football rivalry of the 1940s – that of Cavan and Antrim. It was the counties' third Ulster final meeting in a row and Mick Higgins was surprised with Cavan's 2-12 to 2-4 win.

'We beat Antrim easy that year, which was a bit of a surprise, because Antrim and ourselves were the two big teams in Ulster, and they had beaten us in the final in 1946. They always put it up to us, but that day was probably one of our more comfortable wins against them.'

Sean Gallagher's opening score for Antrim only closed the gap to 0-3 to 0-1, but the Saffrons did catch up when, after Peter Donohoe had stretched Cavan's lead, they found the net. That leveller was cancelled out when Joe Stafford gained a goal for Cavan. The reigning champions tacked on four more points before half-time, while Joe McCallin kicked over two frees for Antrim.

McCallin scored another free two minutes after the break, but Cavan replied with two more of their own. McCallin then scored Antrim's second goal, but they couldn't manage another score. Cavan reeled off two points, the highlight being an overhead effort from Mick Higgins, before Donohoe scored a goal to complete an eight-point victory.

The semi-final against Louth was a very strange game. Stranger still, says Mick Higgins, the final against Mayo was astonishingly similar.

'The semi-final against Louth and the final against Mayo were very similar games. We were leading both by a lot at half-time, then let four goals by in the second half. We definitely had the luck against Louth in the semi-final.'

A gale was blowing down Croke Park on semi-final Sunday against Louth, and Cavan took full advantage, running up 1-9 before Louth scored. Tony Tighe secured Cavan's goal in the twelfth minute. His strike came in the

Edwin Carolan kicks over Cavan's final point in their 1948 All-Ireland semi-final win over Louth

middle of a point-scoring blitz from the Ulster champions. Two Mick Higgins points, a pair of frees from Peter Donohoe (taking his personal tally to 0-6), and another from Edwin Carolan were all registered before Frankie Fagan pointed for Louth in the twenty-fifth minute. Higgins added another before half-time to give Cavan a 1-10 to 0-1 interval lead.

Donohoe put away another free early in the second half, but it was surrounded by a hat-trick of Louth goals from Fagan, Mick Hardy and Ray Mooney, which cut the gap to just four points. Higgins and Fagan swapped scores before Hardy found the net again to leave a point between the teams. Cavan dug in and two Donohoe frees saw them home 1-14 to 4-2.

The heavens conspired to produce almost identical conditions for Cavan's All-Ireland final clash with Mayo. The morning's heavy rain had cleared by the time the game started, but the wind stayed put and, as in the semi-final, blew straight down the pitch.

Over 74,000 turned up at Croke Park for the game and they saw Cavan jump out to a two-point lead after four minutes thanks to a pair of Peter Donohoe frees. Mayo managed to hold Cavan scoreless for the next twenty-three minutes and it looked that the reigning champions had wasted their considerable wind advantage. Then, however, they produced a three-goal bonanza. The first came from Tony Tighe, who executed a one-two with John Joe Cassidy and blasted home. Tighe also provided the finish to Cavan's second goal move, receiving from Joe Stafford before hammering home again.

Tighe turned provider for Cavan's third goal, setting up Victor Sherlock to give the Ulster champions a 3-2 to no score half-time lead.

Cavan lost their shape when centre half-back and captain John Joe O'Reilly left the field shortly after the break. Mayo finally scored when Sean Mulderring pointed, then Peter Solan found the net after J.D. Benson spilled a Padhraic Carney centre.

Cavan shook themselves and pushed back into a twelve-point lead with contributions from Donohoe, Sherlock and a Mick Higgins goal.

Mayo's Tom Acton capitalised on a couple of Cavan defensive lapses to score two goals. Carney narrowed the gap to three points with eleven minutes left when he converted a penalty after a foul on Tom Langan.

John Joe O'Reilly with the Sam Maguire, after leading his men to a successful defence of their title in 1948. Also pictured are trainer Hughie O'Reilly (left) and county chairman Patsy Lynch

Carney and Mongey were running midfield for Mayo, and they both scored points which, along with another from Mulderring, pulled the sides level on 4-4 apiece. Donohoe converted a fourteen-yard free to give Cavan the lead again, but play immediately swung to the other end of the field and Mayo were awarded a fourteen-yard free. Mick Higgins took up position in front of Carney as he prepared to take the free.

'That last play was disputed by Mayo. Padhraic Carney was taking a short free and I blocked it. Mayo maintained I was too close to the ball, but it was at an angle to the goals, and I don't think I was too close. Anyhow, the principal man was the referee and he said it was fair enough, and that was good enough for me.'

Mayo weren't pleased with the amount of added time played either, but the players and supporters had to take their beating. They came back for another one in 1949 against Meath, before the county lifted consecutive All-Ireland titles in 1950 and 1951.

That was for the future: 1948 was Cavan's time to celebrate and John Joe O'Reilly took possession of the Sam Maguire in the more familiar surroundings of Croke Park, after New York the year before.

Cavan's 1948 final-winning team was:

CAVAN 1948		
	J.D. Benson	
Bill Doonan	Brian O'Reilly	Paddy Smith
P.J. Duke	John Joe O'Reilly	Simon Deignan
Victor Sherlock		Phil Brady
Tony Tighe	Mick Higgins	John Joe Cassidy
Joe Stafford	Peter Donohoe	Edwin Carolan
Substitute		
Owen Roe McGovern for John Joe O'Reilly		

In 1949, Cavan steadily made progress towards their three-in-a-row. They enjoyed a twenty-one-point win over Tyrone in the first round of the Ulster championship, then beat Antrim by four points to earn a final spot against Armagh, who just fell short of the reigning champions by a point, 1-7 to 1-6.

The semi-final against Cork was negotiated 1-7 to 2-3, and a record crowd of 79,460 filled Croke Park to see Cavan beat their neighbours Meath and record three consecutive All-Ireland titles. It didn't work out that way, however, as Meath went in 0-7 to 0-3 ahead at the break and held their advantage throughout the second half. Willie Halfpenny found the net for the Leinster champions and, although Mick Higgins replied, Meath held on for a 1-10 to 1-6 win and their first All-Ireland title. The Cavan supporters leaving Croke Park couldn't believe what had happened. According to Higgins, neither could the team.

'It was a shock for us. We thought we had nothing to do to win the All-Ireland but go to Croke Park and pick it up. We really thought we would beat them, but they were all over us in the final. They got a run on us and no matter what we did we couldn't get back into the game. We just didn't click and we were disappointed we didn't make it three-in-a-row, but they beat us fair and square.'

Despite going on to captain Cavan's 1952 All-Ireland winning team, the victory in the Polo Grounds is Mick Higgins' outstanding memory of his years in Cavan's famous blue jersey.

'Going to New York was the thing that I remember most and best. It was a once-off thing that won't be repeated. I suppose you could say it was a bit more special to me because I was born in America, but it didn't make any difference to me where I won it. An All-Ireland is an All-Ireland.'

John Joe O'Reilly

Man of the Match: **John Joe O'Reilly**

With his achievements on the field, John Joe O'Reilly stands alone in the history of Ulster Gaelic football. He played in six All-Ireland finals (1937, 1943, 1945, 1947, 1948 and 1949) and captained Cavan to victories in 1947 and '48, making him the only Ulsterman to lift the Sam Maguire twice, and one of only five men to lead their counties in back-to-back victories. Only a final defeat to Meath in 1949 prevented him from lifting Sam for an unprecedented third year in succession.

His death in 1952, at the age of thirty-four, shocked Ireland and stunned Cavan. He was already regarded in his home county as something of a legend and his early passing only strengthened this feeling.

He was nineteen when he broke into the Cavan senior team after a successful football career at St Patrick's College, where he played on the team that garnered three MacRory Cup successes in a row (in 1935, '36 and '37), assuming the role of captain for two of those victories. He played in his first All-Ireland final in 1937, as Cavan, under the captaincy of his brother 'Big' Tom, drew with Kerry. The Kingdom won the replay by six points.

Five years later he lined out at wing-back, again for his brother Tom, in Cavan's next unsuccessful All-Ireland final appearance. It took a replay to settle things once more and Cavan came up short in the second game, this time to Roscommon.

In 1945, with 'Big' Tom moved to full-back, John Joe took over his brother's centre half-back role, a position at which he would come to be regarded as the best in the history of the game. Cork surprised Cavan in the 1945 final, and John Joe would have to wait another two years before finally claiming an All-Ireland medal. It came in the sweltering heat of New York's Polo Grounds, and he captured his second in the more familiar surroundings of Croke Park a year later.

The reputation he forged during his career meant there was little argument when he was selected at centre half-back in the GAA's centenary team of 1984 and the 'Team of the Millennium' in 2000.

Those who played with him acknowledged him as a born leader who inspired the best in his team-mates, leading the way by word and deed.

Anyone who saw him play or lined up against him spoke of how he could play a man out of the game by concentrating on nothing but the ball. He was an outstanding sportsman in every way.

3

The End of an Era

CAVAN 1952

John Joe O'Reilly leads the Cavan team in the funeral procession of P.J. Duke as it heads up Dublin's O'Connell Street

Cavan gained a measure of revenge over Meath – the county that had denied them a three-in-a-row in 1949 – by beating them in the National League 'home' final the following year. The Breffni men took to the field wearing black armbands and, before the game, a two-minute silence was observed in memory of the recently deceased P.J. Duke.

Duke, who was regarded as one of the best talents in the sport, had played in midfield on the 1947 team, moving to wing-back in 1948. He had won

Sigerson Cup medals with University College Dublin (UCD) in 1945, 1947 and 1949, and had garnered a Railway Cup medal with Ulster less than two months before his death on 1 May 1950. He had died, at the age of twenty-five, after a short illness while at St Vincent's Hospital in Dublin.

His passing provoked a countrywide outpouring of grief. Crowds gathered in O'Connell Street and on the roads back to Cavan to pay their respects. As the cortege made its way down Dublin's main thoroughfare, it was flanked by Duke's team-mates, led by his captain, the great John Joe O'Reilly.

The death of the young player had shaken Cavan, according to Mick Higgins, in much the same way that the death of Cormac McAnallen would shake Tyrone more than fifty years later.

'P.J. was outstanding, a very good right wing-half. He was a real keep fit merchant; he loved it. He was a student at UCD, doing dentistry, and went back down to Dublin. He got pleurisy and because he was fit and strong we thought he could fight it, but he couldn't. Cormac McAnallen seems to have been a very similar sort of person to P.J. Both of them were very fit and took football seriously, and were dedicated to it.'

A lament was quickly penned in honour of the Cavan hero:

New stars may rise in the years before us,
But none like him will they then bethrone,
The boy from Breffni, the pride of Ulster,
God rest you P.J., in sweet Stradone.

 Cavan's win over Meath didn't give them the National League title as 1950 saw the start of an experiment whereby the winners of the 'home' final played New York in the final 'proper'. The visitors from America weren't expected to trouble Cavan, but they ran up a 2-4 to 0-7 lead at half-time, and held on in the second half to record a 2-8 to 0-12 win.

Cavan's championship interest was ended in the Ulster final by Armagh, who won their first provincial title in forty-eight years with a finishing score of 1-11 to 1-7. In 1951 Cavan reached the final again, but fell short of Antrim by a point, 1-7 to 2-3.

By the time the 1952 championship started, many of the players who had won All-Ireland medals in 1947 and 1948, including captain John Joe O'Reilly, had retired. Mick Higgins saw no indication that those same heights would be reached in the season to come.

'There was only Tony Tighe, myself, Phil Brady and Brian O'Reilly left that had won two before. There was also Victor Sherlock and Edwin Carolan who had played in '48. The 1952 team came all of a sudden. We beat Down in Newcastle in the first match, and little did we think at the start of the championship that we would win it out in the end.'

Cavan had no trouble disposing of Down in their opening Ulster championship game. Although the home side initiated the scoring through

Cavan's mighty full-back Phil 'Gunner' Brady clears his lines

John McIlroy, and went ahead again when Martin Walsh made the score 0-2 to 0-1, Cavan powered away as the half wore on. Mick Higgins scored a goal, while Victor Sherlock, Tony Tighe and J.J. Cassidy all picked off points as they ran up an eight-point half-time lead.

Johnny Bashford gave Down a little hope when he fisted in after a goalmouth scramble, but further points and two late goals eased Cavan through 3-10 to 1-3.

Cavan's reward for defeating Down was a shot at settling the score against Antrim, who had beaten them in the previous year's Ulster final. The game at Clones swung from end to end in the opening moments, but the points didn't come until the eleventh minute when Edwin Carolan shot fiercely through a ruck of players and past Mickey Darragh in the Antrim goal. Antrim got on the board a minute later, but Cavan stretched their lead when John Joe Cassidy took a pass from Terry Keoghan and pointed from a narrow angle in the fourteenth minute.

The play continued to be tight and Ray Beirne converted a free for Antrim in the twenty-fourth minute to pull the reigning champions closer, but Tony Tighe finished off a four-man move a minute later for Cavan's second point. This was followed quickly by Cavan's second goal when Seamus Hetherton showed a clean pair of heels to the Antrim defence and drove his shot across Darragh to the corner of the net. Cavan were on a roll and a Cassidy free put them seven points ahead after thirty minutes. In added time Joe Hurley fisted over a point for Antrim to leave the half-time score 2-3 to 0-3 in Cavan's favour.

Cassidy got the second half off to a profitable start with another Cavan point. Antrim could see their crown was slipping and made some positional switches. They immediately reaped the benefit when Sean Gibson was fouled going through and Beirne fired in the penalty to bring the deficit to four points.

Antrim continued to push forward and Kevin Armstrong narrowed the gap with another point six minutes after the goal. Gibson got another to reduce the margin to two points before Cassidy kicked over a free for Cavan to stretch the lead back to a goal. This advantage was almost wiped out when Sean Gallagher crossed for substitute Harry O'Neill to fist goalwards, but Paul Fitzsimons cleared the danger.

It wasn't long, however, before Antrim got their goal and levelled the scores when O'Neill hit the underside of the crossbar with a shot, and Seamus McDonald fisted in the rebound. Cavan were left playing catch-up soon after when Beirne freed the Ulster champions into the lead at 2-6 to 2-5.

Cavan piled forward and, in the fifty-seventh minute, the referee awarded a controversial penalty, which Cassidy converted. Cavan pushed the lead out with a point a minute later and, although seven extra minutes were played, they managed to hold on to book their place in the Ulster final.

The 1952 Ulster semi-final was just the latest in a series of thrilling matches contested between Antrim and Cavan dating from the mid '40s to the early '50s. Most of the time Cavan enjoyed the upper hand but, according to Mick Higgins, there was never much between the sides.

'We were the two outstanding teams in Ulster. Antrim had a great team. They had Kevin Armstrong, Harry O'Neill, Sean Gallagher – great players like that. They were very unlucky to meet us when we were at our best. I think they would have won two or three All-Irelands if we hadn't have beaten them in the north. In 1946, after they had beaten us, they were very unlucky against Kerry in the All-Ireland semi-final.'

In the Ulster final against Monaghan, Cavan enjoyed a rare home advantage as the decider was played at Breffni Park, which had been reopened earlier in the summer after building work.

John Joe Cassidy opened the scoring with a free from the sideline. The lead was doubled when Sherlock won a kick-out, found Carolan, who transferred to Tony Tighe to secure a point. Monaghan pushed forward and Paddy O'Rourke was fouled for a free that Mackie Moyna converted to register their first score.

A Cassidy free and a Seamus Hetherton point, coming within sixty seconds of each other, opened up Cavan's lead by the thirteenth minute. O'Rourke got one back for Monaghan, when he took a pass from Tony Prunty and pointed. Cavan came forward and Liam Maguire, Sherlock and Mick Higgins combined to find Tighe, but the full-forward's shot was stopped on the goal-line by full-back Ollie O'Rourke. Monaghan rallied approaching the break, and two Moyna frees and a Pat Clarke point gave them a 0-5 to 0-4 lead at the interval.

Cavan pressed from the start of the second half and finally got the equaliser when Cassidy freed after Tighe had been fouled in the thirty-seventh minute. Almost immediately, Joe Smith regained the lead for Monaghan before three Cassidy frees in the space of three minutes edged Cavan back ahead.

In the fiftieth minute Moyna hit a free over the post to close the gap, but Cavan's response won them the game. Brian Gallagher's perfect pass found Edwin Carolan, who cut in from the left side to thump to the net. Moyna then tapped over a free to bring his side within a goal. In the remaining minutes, the ball moved from end to end but there were no more scores and Cavan were Ulster champions again.

The All-Ireland semi-final against Cork produced a thrilling finish and a brilliant Cavan comeback. It was a day the Ulster team rode their luck, says man of the match Mick Higgins.

'We ended up winning by a point, but we needed a very good comeback to do it. We were lucky because they were short two of their best men: Eamonn Young, who was injured, and Con McGrath, who was an outstanding midfielder. We had a bit of luck, but they were hard to beat.'

The reason Cork were so hard to beat, according to the *Irish News*, was their over-robust approach to the last quarter of the game. However, the change in tactics was, said the newspaper, also their undoing: 'Cork were tops until they introduced their manhandling tactics, with fatal results.'

Cavan started better, hitting the post and recording a couple of bad wides, before Mick Higgins sent over a free to get the tally rolling in the seventh minute. Tom Moriarty kicked a free to equalise for Cork four minutes later. Victor Sherlock won a ball at midfield and transferred to Higgins, who found Seamus Hetherton to put Cavan back into the lead. There were no more scores until the twenty-fourth minute when Phil Brady caught a 'fifty' from Cork's John Cronin and won a free out. However, the kick was intercepted by Cronin, who fed Moriarty, who met the ball with his fist to punch to the net. Nealy Duggan and Tony Tighe swapped scores as half-time approached, but Denis Kelleher got a point for Cork five minutes into added time at the end of the half, and the Munster champions went in leading 1-3 to 0-3.

Cavan attacked from the whistle and got their reward when John Joe Cassidy hit over a superb point from the wing. Four minutes later Higgins received a free from Paul Fitzsimons and got another point back.

The Cavan squad that brought their county its fifth All-Ireland title in 1952

Cavan were playing well and continued to attack. Sherlock hit a free into the Cork goalmouth and Higgins was fouled for a penalty, but Cassidy's shot was saved by Dan O'Keeffe. Things immediately got worse for Cavan when Jim Cronin crossed for Moriarty to score Cork's second goal in the forty-sixth minute.

Cavan came back, and points from Higgins and Pat Carolan narrowed the gap to two. A Cassidy free brought them level; then the same player collected a break ball and kicked Cavan into the lead, 0-10 to 2-3. Five more minutes were played but Cavan held on to get back into the All-Ireland final.

Neighbours and thwarters of Cavan's 1949 three-in-a-row ambitions, Meath, provided the final opposition. Clashes between the counties were always something special, remembers Mick Higgins.

'We knew each other very well, and there was intense rivalry between Meath and Cavan at the time, especially because both counties had fairly good teams. Any ball you won, any score you got, you earned it. It was tough hard football, but nothing dirty.

'The 1952 final and replay were two dour matches in bad conditions. It was very hard to play football against Meath – they were always a very dogged team, who played a dogged type of football. As long as they kept it out of their own half they were happy.'

Dublin was drenched with incessant rain before the All-Ireland final, and the Croke Park authorities postponed the minor decider between Cavan and Galway to save the pitch for the senior match.

Meath attacked from the throw-in and almost went into an immediate three-point lead, but Paddy Meegan's shot hit the foot of the post and was cleared. In the second minute they did open the scoring, through Jim Reilly.

The crowd sits rapt in attention at the 1952 All-Ireland final between Cavan and Meath

The Leinster champions continued to come forward and Cavan scrambled away a Meath goal chance before opening their account with a goal of their own in the fifth minute, Tony Tighe scoring after being found with a Mick Higgins free. Meath's Peter McDermott was fouled for a free three minutes later. Meegan converted to bring his team within a point of Cavan and, shortly afterwards, he scored from play to equalise. Tighe could have scored two goals, but he palmed the first chance into the hands of grateful Meath keeper Kevin Smith and found the post with the second.

In the sixteenth minute Higgins got Cavan's lead back with a point, but McDermott cut in from the end line to drive over another Meath equaliser. Meath hit a couple of wides before Tighe found Victor Sherlock with a sideline kick, and Cavan were pointed back in front. Meegan won and scored a free for Meath a minute into added time.

There was still time left in the first period for a strange, mini pitch invasion. A fracas in the middle of the pitch prompted a supporter to run onto the field, followed by a member of the clergy. The supporter had a few words with the referee, then both intruders were removed. The teams went in level at the break: Cavan 1-2, Meath 0-5.

After the break Sherlock fed Paul Fitzsimons, who pointed Cavan into the lead. Nine minutes later John Joe Cassidy finished a five-man move with a left foot volley to the net to put Cavan ahead by four. Mattie McDonnell closed the gap to a goal when he fisted over and, in the fifty-second minute, McDermott used his fist to good effect when he met a partial clearance from

A scramble in the Cavan goalmouth during the drawn 1952 All-Ireland final. Meath's famous 'Man in the Cap' Peter McDermott (number 15) waits to pounce

Cavan goalkeeper Seamus Morris to level the scores.

Meath were on the up and, two minutes later, Meegan gave them the lead. Cavan were still trailing a minute into injury-time when Edwin Carolan engineered one of the most bizarre finishes to an All-Ireland final. Looking for a levelling score, Cavan sent the ball towards the Meath goal. Carolan led the chase, but the ball looked favourite to reach the end line. The Meath players gave up the chase and stood up, ready for the kick-out. Carolan collected the ball on the line and kicked it towards the goal from where he stood. His kick, which looked suspiciously like one designed to simply return the ball to the goalkeeper for a kick-out, dropped over the bar off the far post and was signalled a point. Cavan had escaped with a draw and Mick Higgins knew it.

'I was forty yards away, so I couldn't tell if it was wide or not. If he was going for a point it was a ridiculous thing to try, it was bad football. It's always bad football when someone on the end line tries for a point instead of kicking it in towards the goal to one of your own men, and he was nearly at the flag. The umpire said it wasn't wide and the Meath goalkeeper Kevin Spence said it was. I'll bow to the umpire on that one.'

The weather wasn't much better two weeks later when a record 62,515 crowd turned out for the replay. The postponed minor final acted as the

Cavan's Seamus Hetherton jumps for the ball with his Meath marker in the 1952 final

curtain-raiser, but the Cavan followers in the crowd were disappointed by their county's 2-9 to 1-6 loss to Galway.

The senior game raised more cheers for Cavan supporters, as they convincingly beat Meath. Mick Higgins played a winning captain's role, scoring seven of Cavan's nine points. Although he was honoured to captain his county, it made little difference to how he approached the game.

'You never passed much remarks about being captain. What we used to do in Cavan at that time was to make the longest serving member on the team captain. In 1952 that just happened to be me. You didn't do much, you just called the coin toss and decided what way you were playing.'

Higgins won the toss, and pointed a free after three minutes. This was to give Cavan a lead they lost just once in the game. Higgins added another free five minutes later but, with both sides struggling in the conditions, no more scores were registered until Mattie McDonnell finally got Meath's first point after twenty-three minutes. Tony Tighe restored Cavan's two-point lead and, just before half-time, Jim Reilly scored Meath's second point to leave the interval score 0-3 to 0-2 in Cavan's favour.

Meath started the second half better and Peter McDermott got their equalising point eight minutes in. Then, Edwin Carolan was hauled down in front of goal and Higgins kicked the free to give Cavan the lead they held

The ball evades the chasing pack during the 1952 final replay between Cavan and Meath

until the final whistle. Johnny Cusack got another Cavan point, which was responded to by McDermott, who got Meath their fourth. Higgins then converted a free to keep Cavan's noses in front. While Higgins was enjoying a superb day from placed balls, Meath captain Paddy Meegan was enduring a terrible afternoon. When Brian Smith took over as free taker, he fared little better.

Higgins kicked another free, and popped over two more in the fifty-eighth and fifty-ninth minutes. Meath gained a consolation point in the third minute of injury time, but Cavan weren't going to be denied their deserved win.

The delighted Cavan supporters poured onto the pitch and subjected their captain Mick Higgins to what the *Irish News* called 'very enthusiastic, yet embarrassing' attentions. He didn't mind that, or the other task of a winning captain – lifting the Sam Maguire. Indeed, seven days previously he didn't think he would even play.

'For a time I didn't think I would get to lift the Cup because the week before the match I had spent three days in bed with the flu. But everything just went right for me. There are days when you would be totally fit and nothing goes right, but that day I was lucky enough that everything went right.'

Cavan's fifth All-Ireland winning team was:

CAVAN 1948		
	Seamus Morris	
Jim McCabe	Phil Brady	Des Maguire
Paddy Carolan	Liam Maguire	Brian O'Reilly
	Victor Sherlock	Tom Hardy
Seamus Hetherton	Mick Higgins	Edwin Carolan
John Joe Cassidy	Tony Tighe	Johnny Cusack
Substitute		
Paul Fitzsimons for John Joe Cassidy		

After being denied three-in-a-row by Meath in 1949, it was especially sweet to bring the Sam Maguire through the royal county and back to Cavan to the joyous welcome the people always afforded their All-Ireland champions.

'You always got a great reception with twenty thousand or thirty thousand people. Money was scarce at that time, and people didn't throw it around, so it was great that they would come out to welcome you home with the Cup. They lived for football – there wasn't really anything else, especially in Cavan. If you won an All-Ireland it was celebrated for days afterwards.'

The celebrations had barely died down when Cavan's most famous footballing son, Commandant John Joe O'Reilly, died at the Curragh Military Hospital on 21 November. He had been in hospital to undergo an operation for a kidney complaint, but never woke up after the surgery. He was thirty-four years old.

John Joe's funeral procession traced the same path that P.J. Duke's had taken only two years before, travelling through Dublin and Meath, and into his beloved Cavan. Fittingly, this was also the path that Cavan's heroes took when returning victorious from Croke Park. The cortege of more than two miles followed the coffin north, pausing at Breffni Park in Cavan town, before moving on to John Joe's home village of Killeshandra. His body was carried to the grave by his team-mates and buried with full military honours.

More than fifty years after his death, John Joe was selected at centre half-back in the GAA's centenary and millennium teams. Mick Higgins feels that all the accolades were well deserved.

'John Joe's death had a big effect on Cavan football because they were looking forward to him to train the team. He was very dedicated, and was always super fit at a time when there wouldn't have been as much interest in the fitness side of things. He was a very clean footballer. He never hit a man, even with his shoulder; he played the ball the whole time. He started at centre-field, then moved to centre half-back, but he was the type of footballer who could have played anywhere.

'He had great control. When he got possession, he never just kicked it away: he always placed it. Tony Tighe and myself were in the forward line and we were always sure that if he kicked the ball to us it would get to us. He was a very intelligent footballer.'

As with P.J. Duke, John Joe O'Reilly's passing encouraged some to put pen to paper to compose a lyrical tribute in his memory:

> *We bless and keep you in our prayers, may He count you with His own,*
> *While Ulster mourns your passing from the Ards to Inishowen,*
> *God rest and keep you John Joe and we pray for you today,*
> *When Cavan lost their bravest man on a cold November day.*

Cavan surrendered their Ulster and All-Ireland titles in the 1953 provincial final against Armagh, and have not appeared in an All-Ireland final since. Indeed, since 1952, Cavan have won the Ulster senior title just seven times, compared to the thirty-two titles they gained up to and including the year of their last All-Ireland. Their decline in fortune has been remarkable given their previous success, but the teams Mick Higgins played on in the '40s and early '50s are still remembered as some of the best that Gaelic football has produced.

'Peter Donohoe, Tony Tighe and myself played with the same club, Mountnugent. Donohoe was full-forward, Tighe was right three-quarter and I was centre three-quarter. Between club games, the county and Ulster in the Railway Cup, we played most of our matches together.

'At the back you had John Joe, Simon Deignan and P.J. Duke, and they were an outstanding half-back line. Billy Doonan was good in the full-back line and then you had Victor Sherlock and Phil Brady, who were two outstanding footballers at midfield. Edwin Carolan was a good corner-forward and we had other good players too. We had really good all-around teams and were just short maybe one or two players. The only way to win an All-Ireland is to have a good all-around team with a few outstanding footballers thrown in.'

Mick Higgins

Man of the Match: **Mick Higgins**
Mick Higgins won All-Ireland medals with Cavan in 1947 and 1948, the first of which was garnered in his New York birthplace. However, it was the part he played in captaining the county to their fifth title in 1952 that secured his place in Breffni football folklore.

Born in America to a Mayo father and Cavan mother, he returned to Ireland when he was five years of age, and enjoyed his first football success in 1938 when he helped St Mary's of Dundalk win the MacRory Cup. His next bout of serious football was also played outside Cavan borders when, while working in Kildare, he was in the 'lily-whites' minor team beaten in the 1940 Leinster final.

Two years later he was back in Cavan and, in 1943, he made the step up to the county senior team, quickly establishing a reputation as one of the best forwards in the game.

He played as wing-forward in the 1943 team beaten by Roscommon in that year's All-Ireland final, but missed the Ulstermen's surprise loss to Cork two years later due to injury. He orchestrated Cavan's victories in 1947 and 1948 from centre half-forward, and scored Cavan's crucial second goal at the Polo Grounds.

As captain in 1952, he steered Cavan through two tight, dour contests with neighbours Meath in the All-Ireland final and replay. After a 2-4 to 1-7 draw in the first game, Higgins proved the hero in the replay, scoring seven of Cavan's nine points – six of which were from frees – on a terrible day that made every placed ball a challenge. While Meath captain Paddy Meegan struggled with his kicking, missing a number of chances, Higgins was consistently accurate, ensuring the Sam Maguire would return to Cavan. Holding the trophy aloft at the final whistle was just the icing on the cake in a brilliant career.

4

'Thanks, Offaly'

DOWN 1960, 1961

Of all that places that can lay claim to playing a part in the development of one of the best Gaelic football teams the sport has ever seen, the home of English soccer seems an unlikely candidate. Nevertheless, Wembley stadium looms large in the legend of Down's history-making All-Ireland winning teams of 1960 and 1961.

The London county board had established the Whitsun Tournament in 1958. The qualifying games were staged in Ireland, but the last two teams battled for the tournament title on the hallowed turf at Wembley. The experience of playing in the first final must have done Derry some good because, despite being beaten by Galway in London, they succeeded in lifting

The five men who brought Sam back to the Mourne county (from left to right): Joe Lennon, D.J. Kane, Paddy O'Rourke, Paddy Doherty and Kevin Mussen

their first Ulster title and made it to the All-Ireland final later that year.

The following year a last minute Paddy Doherty point beat Derry in the play-off to earn Down a trip to London for the final against Galway. Kevin Mussen led the Mournemen out on 10 May 1959 and, in front of 32,000 supporters, Down beat Galway 3-9 to 4-4. A new footballing power was emerging and the Wembley spectators were the first to get a glimpse of its potential. Down went on to win their first Ulster title that year, and became the first team to bring the Sam Maguire across the border twelve months later.

 At the 1950 county convention in Warrenpoint a senior football league was established that ensured regular competition and contact between the best players in Down. A selection committee was also set up, comprising five to seven people charged with picking the Down team rather than, as had previously been the custom, letting the whole county committee have its say. That had often led to conflict, as well as reluctance to pick the best senior team for fear of weakening the county's junior selection by rendering some players ineligible.

The decision to put the senior team's interests ahead of everything else paid dividends, says Ballykinlar's Paddy Doherty, who would become one of the greatest Gaelic footballers of all time.

'I had played along with James McCartan and Tony Hadden on a Down junior team. We would have won the junior All-Ireland but the decision was made to bring us all on to the senior team and, in 1958, Derry beat us in the Ulster final.'

Doherty is in no doubt over who was chiefly responsible for setting Down on the path that would take them to the pinnacle of Gaelic football.

'Maurice Hayes was the main man. Maurice looked after all of the players and worried about everybody else after that. We didn't get much for winning, but we were looked after. There was no such thing as All-Stars or anything like that, and we didn't get what players would get now, but we were looked after.'

Hayes, who was to go on to become an important figure in the Northern Ireland civil service as well as a respected author was, in 1956, the first secretary of the all-county league. That same year, he was appointed county secretary. At the time of Down's 1958 Ulster final appearance – their first since 1940, and only their second overall – Hayes, alongside former players Barney Carr and Brian Denvir, took their places on the newly-established senior selection committee who were tasked with paving Down's way to an All-Ireland final.

When Down beat Carlow 3-5 to 2-7 in an April 1956 challenge match, it was clear that a promising team was taking shape. Nine of the Down team on show that day would go on to win All-Ireland medals four years later. The McKenna Cup campaign saw the addition of a young corner-back called James McCartan and a promising centre-forward named Joe Lennon. They were still some way from the finished article, however, and endured a disappointing championship exit to Donegal in 1957. The triumvirate of Hayes, Carr and Denvir got to work in 1958 and guided Down to the Ulster final where they lost by three points to Derry.

They gained a modicum of revenge the next year when they beat Derry in the play-off for the Wembley tournament. Their Whitsun final victory over Galway made counties outside Ulster sit up and take notice. Down's first Ulster final win, a 2-16 to 0-7 hammering of Cavan, confirmed their new status. A first All-Ireland semi-final followed, but they couldn't match Galway, who won 1-11 to 1-4. The team didn't like the feeling of losing at Croke Park and decided that 1960 would be different. Paddy Doherty recalls:

'We knew that in 1959 we hadn't shown anything against Galway in the All-Ireland semi-final, and they beat us well. But we talked it over and decided among ourselves that we would be back the next year and would win the All-Ireland.'

In 1960 Down won the Lagan Cup, the Ulster section of the National League, before defeating Kerry with a superb performance in the league semi-final. Cavan provided the final opposition and Down lifted its first national trophy with a 0-12 to 0-9 win.

Down again travelled to Wembley, and again beat Galway, with Patsy O'Hagan scoring a stunning hat-trick in a 4-11 to 3-7 win. Sean O'Neill and Paddy Doherty were Down's other standouts in a brilliant performance.

'It was great to play at Wembley,' says Doherty. 'The first year I played at Wembley I was living in Woolwich at the time. We played at Wembley four times and won four times. Patsy O'Hagan scored three of the best goals he ever scored in his life at Wembley.'

Playing at the famous London venue was a particular thrill for Doherty, who had toyed with becoming a soccer player before committing to Ballykinlar and Down.

'I had been playing football for Ballykinlar, then I went for a trial at Lincoln City and stayed for eight weeks, but came home again. I signed for Ballyclare Comrades and scored thirty-three goals in one season from outside left, but I wanted to get back to the Gaelic. I couldn't stand just watching my club at home and I always wanted to play in an All-Ireland final rather than an Irish Cup final.'

Down made the most of the gale at their backs during the first half of their Ulster championship opener against Antrim at Casement Park, and racked up 0-11 while their hosts couldn't manage a single point in thirty minutes of football. Down grasped just three more points after the break, but Antrim could only record 1-4, and Down moved on to the Ulster semi-final.

The horrible weather in Dungannon was the main talking point of Down's semi-final win over Monaghan. Around 7,000 hardy souls turned up to get a drenching and see Down lead 1-4 to 0-5 at half-time without breaking into a jog. James McCartan scored Down's goal and found the net again in the second half, as they eased away from a game but overmatched Monaghan team. The right flank of Monaghan's defence was under particular

Cavan's Sean Conaty beats Down's Pat Rice to a high centre during the Ulster final played at Clones on 1 August 1960

pressure, as Paddy Doherty and Brian Morgan ran them ragged and combined for 0-6.

Just before the Down minors took to St Tiernach's Park in Clones to beat Monaghan in the Ulster final, a heavy shower soaked the ground and the rain continued to fall throughout the afternoon. Cavan provided Down's senior opposition as the Mournemen bid to retain their provincial title for a second year. They started about it the right way as Dan McCartan, Kevin Mussen and Sean O'Neill combined to give Paddy Doherty the chance to thump in a goal just forty seconds after the throw-in. Less than a minute later James McCartan found the net. When Doherty tapped over a free soon after, all the indications were that Down would be putting rout to Cavan in the two teams' second successive Ulster final.

The Breffni men managed to stem the bleeding, however, and in the thirteenth minute, opened their account when Con Smith found the net. Sean O'Neill pointed a free for Down, but Cavan were gaining the upper hand at midfield and Eamonn McKay was forced to save well at close range from Smith. Smith added a point to his opening strike, and another from Brady pulled Cavan to within a goal, 1-2 to 2-2 at the break.

Cavan continued their better form into the second half and Smith chipped away with frees, his third of the half drawing Cavan level six minutes after the break. Down's Ulster crown was wobbling, but they had another card to play. Tony Hadden moved to midfield from the right corner of the attack, with Joe Lennon going the other direction, and the switch immediately began to pay off. Midfield was settled, and Doherty and O'Neill were able to take the lead back for Down with a free each.

Cavan still threatened, however, and McKay saved smartly from Charlie Gallagher. McKay's save set in motion the move that won the game, as Dan McCartan came out of defence with the ball, found Hadden, who passed to Mussen. Mussen got the ball in to Doherty, who thumped past Brian O'Reilly in the Cavan goal. Brian Morgan took Sean O'Neill's pass and fisted over a point to stretch the lead to six. Con Smith pointed for Cavan, but scores from Hadden and Jarlath Carey made the game safe. Jim McDonnell's

final two points were little consolation for Cavan, and Down took their second Ulster title with a 3-7 to 1-8 win.

A brand new All-Ireland finalist was assured in 1960 as Down's opponents, Offaly, had just won their first Leinster crown. Down weren't entirely sure what they would get from the mostly unknown Offaly team. What they did get was the fright of their lives.

Backed by a strong breeze, the Leinster champions jumped into a three-point lead after ten minutes. Their third point could have been a goal, but Eamonn McKay saved from Tommy Greene before Sean Ryan knocked over the rebound. It was McKay's second important save after thwarting Sean Brererton before a point was on the board.

Down finally pointed through Patsy O'Hagan, and Paddy Doherty steadied the ship further when he kicked over from Sean O'Neill's pass.

Mick Casey garnered Offaly's fourth point, but Doherty replied when he won and scored a free. In the nineteenth minute Down had a lucky escape when a drive from Har Donnelly shaved the outside of the post, but McKay's goal didn't stay intact for long. Four minutes later Sean Ryan booted a sideline kick towards the Down goal, which Casey gathered and fired past McKay. Offaly were four points ahead and continued to press forward. Their reward came when, just before half-time, Donnelly managed to get the final touch in a goalmouth scramble. When the whistle went, Down trailed 2-4 to 0-3 and were in big trouble.

Down at least had the wind advantage in the second half and began purposefully, although James McCartan put a good chance wide before Doherty registered their fourth point. Joe Lennon won the kick-out and fed

The Cavan team before their 1950 National League 'home' final victory over Meath.
The squad took to the field in black armbands in memory of P.J. Duke, who had died on 1 May that year

John Joe O'Reilly (near) leads Cavan around the pitch before the 1947 All-Ireland semi-final against Roscommon

Armagh's Oisin McConville skips past Dublin's Paul Casey during the 2002 All-Ireland semi-final

Kieran McGeeney won't let Kerry's Eoin Brosnan stop him during the 2002 All-Ireland final

Paul McGrane rises highest in a midfield tussle during his side's battle with Kerry for Sam

Joe Kernan lifts Sam, his assistant Paul Grimley by his side

Brian McGuigan doesn't let a bit of shirt-pulling from Eamon Fitzmaurice hold him back during the 2003 All-Ireland semi-final against Kerry

No holds were barred in the first ever all-Ulster All-Ireland final. Philip Jordan, ball in hand, hits the deck with Armagh's Paddy McKeever close at hand

Conor Gormley achieves legendary status in Tyrone football history as he goes flat out and blocks Steven McDonnell's attempt at goal, sealing Peter Canavan's men's All-Ireland title

Cormac McAnallen couldn't contain his joy after Tyrone's All-Ireland victory. This picture took up the entire front page of the Irish News *the day following the final, and again just over five months later, the day after Cormac died*

O'Hagan, who further narrowed the deficit. Doherty scored a free for Down and added another point to take the shortfall to within a goal, 2-4 to 0-7, five minutes into the half. Offaly put the brakes on Down's comeback with two points, the first a Donnelly free, the second from Tommy Greene.

Doherty scored Down's eighth point, then the ninth, when he finished a move involving Kevin Mussen and Joe Lennon. Down kept pushing for goal and Paddy McCormack had to be alert to snuff out James McCartan, while goalkeeper Willie Nolan saved from Tony Hadden and twice from Brian Morgan.

Then referee Tom Cunningham threw Down a lifeline when he awarded James McCartan a penalty after a passage of play that could have easily ended with a free-out against McCartan. Offaly still led by three points as Paddy Doherty, in the middle of a brilliant performance, stepped up to take the kick.

'I can safely say that was my best ever game. We were struggling and were three points down with six minutes to go. We got a penalty and I had to score it.'

Willie Dolan had no chance as the ball took off from Doherty's left foot and flew into the net to level the scores at Down 1-9, Offaly 2-6.

Two minutes later Tony Hadden finished a run from midfield by fisting over to put Down ahead for the first time. Donnelly brought Offaly back level with a free, and a chaotic last few minutes saw both sides miss chances. Leo Murphy made a timely intervention to prevent Brererton winning it for Offaly, while Paddy Doherty, who finished with a magnificent tally of 1-7, hit the post from an acute angle and the ball bounced wide. Even without the winning score, Doherty had put on a spectacular display. Without him, said the *Irish News*, 'Down would have fared disastrously'.

After the close call against Offaly, the Down management felt something new needed to be done, so they enlisted the services of Meath's Peter McDermott, a double All-Ireland winner in 1949 and 1954, when he was team captain. McDermott had been joint-trainer with Down's All-Ireland winning 1946 junior team, and had been involved with the Newry Shamrocks club. While he was unsure that the new young stars of Gaelic football would want to listen to him, Paddy Doherty believes that McDermott's input was just what the team needed.

'We thought we were unbeatable, but we struggled a bit against Offaly in the semi-final. Peter came in and told us that we were going for an All-Ireland and we would have to give a lot more. It was do or die.'

A record crowd of just over 68,000 filed into Croke Park for the replay. Both sides missed chances before Patsy O'Hagan opened the scoring and then created the chance for Joe Lennon to increase the tally after five minutes.

Three minutes later Offaly roared back when a Charlie Wren sideline ball from forty-five yards found the net. Soon after, Tommy Cullen doubled the lead with a point. Like the first game, Offaly's goal spurred them into action and Down had a let-off when Har Donnelly struck it wide of their net. After thirteen minutes Donnelly sent a free between the posts to give the Leinster champions a three-point lead. Sean Brererton recorded another point from the right wing for Offaly and both sides missed chances as the game became increasingly scrappy. Patsy O'Hagan forced a point-blank save from Willie Dolan just before the break, and Offaly went in 1-3 to 0-2 ahead.

Down hadn't played well, but started a lot better after the resumption, with O'Hagan just missing a goal, his shot hitting the outside of the post. Despite Down's bright start, Offaly scored next when Donnelly converted a twenty-one yard free. Down had registered four wides before O'Neill ran at the defence and fed to James McCartan, whose score got his side off the mark in the second half. McCartan kept the comeback rolling with another point while Tony Hadden fired over from long range for another.

In the forty-fifth minute James McCartan won possession and punted forward to Sean O'Neill. O'Neill managed to get the ball to O'Hagan, whose shot was saved by Nolan; but the goalkeeper couldn't hold it, and Brian Morgan followed in to punch a goal that put Down ahead, 1-5 to 1-4.

Rain started to pour down and the wind, which was backing the Mournemen, got up. With eleven minutes left, McCartan soloed through and scored. A Doherty free stretched Down's lead to three and, although Tommy Greene replied for Offaly, it wasn't enough as Down held on and their jubilant supporters charged onto the pitch.

Down was in its first All-Ireland final and, as a result, interest in the big day reached unprecedented levels all over the country. Croke Park received 80,000 applications for 20,000 stand tickets while an advertisement appeared in the *Armagh Observer* from a Tyrone man offering a three-and-a-half acre farm for ten tickets.

The final fever in the county itself hit the team when they found their training sessions attended by hundreds of spectators. 'Everywhere,' remembers Paddy Doherty, 'was red and black.'

Peter McDermott returned to the camp to help out in the fortnight between the semi-final replay and the final. Their opponents, Kerry, as reigning champions, with another nineteen All-Irelands under their belt, didn't need any Meath men to tell them what to expect on the big day. It all made for the perfect final experience.

'That year we had thirty-one counties cheering for us to beat Kerry,' says Doherty. 'To win the All-Ireland for the first time you really have to beat Kerry to do it right. They are the best and it's special to beat them.'

The Croke Park gates opened at noon on Sunday, 25 September, but crowds had been gathering for two hours before that. When the gates were closed at 2.15pm, just under 88,000 people had managed to squeeze into the ground. Thousands more were turned away disappointed.

The Down players had journeyed to Dublin from their homes that morning. Every Down All-Ireland final team since has followed their example.

The first year we went down to Dublin, in 1959, we went to Butlin's and stayed there, and then went down to Dublin on the morning of the game.

Down captain Kevin Mussen grasps for Sam in a special mock-up spread in the Irish News *on the eve of the 1960 All-Ireland final*

SEE INSIDE

Down have will to win ... Page 2

Pen Pictures of the Teams .... Page 3

Down Captain clears the way for the Sam Maguire .... Page 4

After that we didn't stay down, we stayed at home. We slept in our own beds, went to Newry, got a police escort to the border, then a garda escort to wherever we were going to stay before the match.

'We didn't realise the crowds were as big as they were. We didn't know anything about it because we were in the hotel and didn't go into Croke Park until half two or three o'clock. Even then, we went in the back road.'

Down were first on the pitch, and Kevin Mussen led them out to a deafening reception.

Down's Kevin O'Neill tussles with the two Kerry forwards Garry McMahon and Seamus Murphy as his team-mate Pat Rice waits for the outcome

Kerry, familiar with the All-Ireland final ritual, followed behind captain Paudie Sheehy.

They roared into their inexperienced opponents from the start, but the Down defence turned back the Kingdom's first three attacks. George Lavery broke up the last of these, and his kick found Tony Hadden, who opened the scoring with a fine solo effort after two minutes. Mick O'Connell forced a save from Eamonn McKay before equalising for Kerry. McKay saved from O'Connell again, then Patsy O'Hagan put Paddy Doherty through, but Doherty saw his shot cannon off the post and cleared. It was the definition of end-to-end stuff, and Tadhg Lyne gave Kerry the lead from a free after Mussen had fouled the ball. Joe Lennon equalised after fourteen minutes, and Doherty kicked Down into the lead from a free soon after. Within little over a minute, an O'Neill free and a point from James McCartan stretched Down's lead to a goal. Hadden scored Down's sixth point with fifteen minutes of the first half gone.

Lyne closed the gap with two frees for Kerry, but Doherty pushed it open again with a free in the twenty-second minute. Approaching half-time, another Lyne free made the score at the break Down 0-7, Kerry 0-5.

Kerry had the wind advantage in the second half and a point from Mick O'Connell soon after the restart shaved the difference to one. Paudie Sheehy shot just wide before Seamus Murphy levelled things at 0-7 each. Kerry were coming back, but Down would outscore the Kingdom 2-2 in the rest of the game.

Kerry pile on the pressure as Down goalkeeper Eamonn McKay and full-back Leo Murphy fight to protect their goal

Kevin Mussen aimed a sideline kick at James McCartan, who sent a high lob towards goal from forty yards out. It headed straight for goalkeeper Johnny Culloty's hands but, when he reached up, the ball squirmed out of his grip and into the net. It was the break that Down needed, says Paddy Doherty.

'It really could have went any way. We got a lucky break when James lobbed a high ball in which deceived Johnny Culloty and went into the net. The first half was even and we led by four points, but Kerry came back into it and levelled it. Then we got that lucky goal.'

A minute later McCartan found Sean O'Neill in the right corner and O'Neill moved the ball to the in-rushing Doherty. Tim Lyons could do nothing but foul Doherty in the square and referee John Dowling had no alternative but to award the penalty. Doherty picked himself up and prepared to take the kick that would probably seal Down's first All-Ireland win. He didn't mind the pressure because he didn't feel it.

'There was no pressure because I was playing well enough. Lucky enough it won us the game. I took the one against Offaly when it really mattered. The one against Kerry wasn't any bigger than that one.'

Doherty's fiercely struck kick gave Down a six-point lead, which Kerry couldn't pull back. The final minutes brought just one Kerry score and three for Down, all from Paddy Doherty's boot. The last, a superb overhead kick, was the exclamation point on Down's great day.

The Down supporters couldn't wait to celebrate and a whistle heralding a 'fifty' precipitated a mini pitch invasion which was cleared just long enough for John Dowling to blow the real full-time whistle and put the official stamp on Down's 2-10 to 0-8 victory.

Down's history-making team was:

DOWN 1960		
	Eamonn McKay	
George Lavery	Leo Murphy	Pat Rice
Kevin Mussen	Dan McCartan	Kevin O'Neill
Joe Lennon		Jarlath Carey
Sean O'Neill	James McCartan	Paddy Doherty
Tony Hadden	Patsy O'Hagan	Brian Morgan

Substitute
Kieran Denvir for Lennon

The supporters returned to the field and swept their heroes up in a wave of sheer joy. That took its toll, according to Paddy Doherty.

'We got more abuse after it was over than we had during the match. Everybody was trying to carry you and get a hold of you.'

Captain Kevin Mussen was lifted and carried to the Hogan Stand where he raised the Sam Maguire to thunderous cheering and applause. The Down supporters claimed Croke Park as their own, and one Mourne patriot scaled the goalposts at the Hill 16 end and hoisted a red and black flag.

When the Down followers finally tore themselves away from the scene of their county's historic victory, they spilled onto the streets of Dublin and celebrated long into the night. The next day they lined the streets to acclaim their heroes as they made for home. The road through Meath and Louth was lined with red and black flags, and Paddy Doherty enjoyed the return journey as it crawled north.

Kevin Mussen receives the Sam Maguire after the 1960 final

'We stopped over in Dublin that night and set off at about ten o'clock on Monday morning. We went as far as Gormanston, where Joe Lennon was a teacher, and went into the college and showed the Cup around. We got to Drogheda; we walked over the Boyne with the Cup.

'We came to Dundalk, where we got a civic reception. We went into a hotel and had a meal. That was about

midnight or one in the morning. We didn't get into the Slieve Donard until half three on Tuesday morning.'

Before they got to Newcastle, there was the small matter of taking the Sam Maguire across the border for the first time. At the customs post at Carrickarnon, the officer on duty gave the party one instruction: 'Now you have it, see you keep it.'

Sam was in the north, but not yet in Down, and the biggest reception awaited the team in Newry.

'The crowds were everywhere; there must have been 40,000 people in Newry. We really knew then that we had won it. After Newry we stopped and had a civic reception in Downpatrick, and a torchlight procession, before we headed into Newcastle. Everything had changed; we were looked on as heroes. It was great.'

Down had had another successful trip to Wembley – where they put on a commanding display to rip Kerry apart, 4-5 to 1-7 – by the time they lined out to face Fermanagh in the first round of the 1961 Ulster championship. The match against Fermanagh produced a different type of encounter.

There wasn't much flowing football in evidence. Although Fermanagh succeeded in getting a 0-3 to 0-2 advantage midway through the first half, Down managed to step up a gear. While still performing a long way below their best, they outscored their opponents 0-7 to 0-1 for the rest of the half. After the break, things started to turn unsavoury as niggle set in and

Fermanagh adopted a more physical approach towards their clearly superior opponents. The football didn't get any better and Down finished 0-12 to 0-7 ahead at the end of sixty dour minutes.

The Ulster semi-final marked Down's third meeting with Derry that year, after the Mournemen had avenged a Lagan Cup final defeat by beating Derry in the McKenna Cup semi-final. The game at Casement Park saw Down produce a memorable performance – so memorable that the *Frontier Sentinel* declared:

'If the 15 gallant Down men who represented their illustrious county in the Ulster Senior Football Championship semi-final at Casement Park against Derry never kicked another ball, they would have done enough in one game to ensure for many years to come that their names would live in the memory of those who witnessed the game.'

Derry's Denis McKeever started the scoring, but Down made a quick reply when Jarlath Carey soloed through and played the ball into the square, which James McCartan finished to the net. Derry replied with a goal of their own soon after when McKeever crossed for Brian Rafferty to score. Leo Murphy converted a 'fifty' for Down and two quick-fire points followed from Sean O'Neill and Tony Hadden. Down pressed home their advantage through Paddy Doherty, who scored a point, then a goal, after taking the pass from O'Neill. Doherty followed his goal with another point before Derry scored three of the half's final four points to leave the score at the break 2-7 to 1-4 in Down's favour.

After the restart a Sean O'Connell free and a point from Leo O'Neill narrowed the gap to four points, but two from Doherty – the first a free – stretched Down back into a six-point lead. Derry, with little to lose, started to pour forward and, inspired by Jim McKeever, they nibbled at Down's advantage point by point. Just three separated the sides when Phil Stuart bore down on Eamonn McKay's goal, but the Down keeper preserved his side's lead with a stunning save. Derry's best chance was gone and, in the final two minutes, a Sean O'Neill free and an O'Hagan point completed the scoring with Down 2-12 to 1-10 ahead.

Down returned to Casement Park for an Ulster final meeting with Armagh. Missing James McCartan, who had injured his shoulder in the Derry game, they were given the runaround by a determined Armagh side for much of the first half. Brian Morgan opened the scoring for Down with their second attack. A Pat Campbell free levelled for Armagh and, in the eighth minute, Kevin Halfpenny gave them a 0-2 to 0-1 lead. Down had a lucky escape when Mick McQuaid almost found the net for Armagh as he fisted against the foot of Eamonn McKay's post. Both sides had chances and McKay saved well from Harry Loughran before Halfpenny added a point in the eighteenth minute, then another, to increase Armagh's advantage. Brian Morgan wiped it out when he found the net in the twentieth minute. McQuaid restored Armagh's lead when he forced the ball past McKay after a goalmouth scramble. The sides swapped points and Morgan fired against the bar for Down, but two Armagh frees gave them a five-point half-time lead, 1-7 to 1-2.

At half-time, Kevin Mussen made way for James McCartan, and the game changed.

'We started the Ulster final that day without James,' says Paddy Doherty. 'He came on at half-time and we had been getting it tight from Armagh. The first ball I lobbed in, James fisted it to the net. That was the difference he made for us.'

Three frees from Doherty soaked up the deficit before he found McCartan on the right.

The substitute fired against the post, then gathered the rebound and scored a goal. Doherty hit the post with a free before converting one; then Sean O'Neill scored to swell the lead. P.J. McElroy fired Down four points ahead, although McQuaid got Armagh scoring again with a free. Doherty kicked over Down's ninth point from a placed ball. A McQuaid free and a point from Harry Hoy kept things close, and Armagh thought they had a goal when another goalmouth scramble resulted in Jimmy Whan forcing the ball into the net. However, it was disallowed and Doherty tapped over another free. Down held on to a three-point lead and their Ulster title.

The repeat of the previous year's All-Ireland final pairing made for a highly anticipated semi-final clash with Kerry. The Kingdom was keen for revenge while the Down side was equally eager to prove their 1960 win wasn't a fluke.

Sean O'Neill got Down off to the best possible start when he took a pass from Jarlath Carey and opened the scoring with a goal. Kerry hit back from the kick-out and John Dowling passed to Timmy O'Sullivan, who knocked over Kerry's first point. James McCartan scored a free for Down and O'Sullivan got Kerry's next two points, the first created by Mick O'Connell, the second by Teddy O'Dowd. The sides swapped quick-fire wides before Paddy Doherty scored after Lennon and O'Neill had made the running. Tony Hadden quickly added another after a clearance from John Smith.

Down were on top at midfield, with Joe Lennon especially good, and Doherty added their next point with fifteen minutes on the clock. The Ulster champions kept coming and a lengthy clearance out of defence was gathered by P.J. McElroy, who scored another point for Down. Kerry stopped Down's assault and started one of their own when O'Connell combined with John Dowling to set up O'Dowd for a point. Seven minutes from half-time Kerry brought the difference between the two teams to a goal and Mick O'Dwyer kept up the pressure with two frees. Just before the interval Dan McAuliffe equalised to leave the board reading Kerry 0-8, Down 1-5.

At the restart Doherty got the lead back for Down, a lead they never lost. James McCartan found Brian Morgan, who doubled the advantage; then Tony Hadden was illegally impeded going through on goal and Down were awarded a penalty. Down supporters readied themselves to salute the inevitable goal that Paddy Doherty would provide from the spot. It didn't happen, as Doherty miskicked his shot to Johnny Culloty in the Kerry goal. It was a rare event that, unsurprisingly, dominates Doherty's memories of the day.

'Missing the penalty is the one thing I really remember about that game. I kicked the ground before the ball, but managed to score three points after it and we won.'

Down might have regretted the missed penalty more, says Doherty, if Kerry hadn't moved Timmy O'Sullivan back to deal with him.

'Kerry played well that day, especially in the first half. Their best forward was on Dan McCartan and he had scored three points, but I was playing well in the half-forward line and they moved him back to mark me. That finished the Kerry forward line.'

Hadden fisted over his team's eighth point to stretch their advantage to a goal. Burke narrowed things to two points but his effort proved to be Kerry's last score. With seven minutes left Doherty recovered his form by soloing through and scoring Down's ninth point. Three minutes later he took a ball from James McCartan and put it over, then smacked over a brilliant sideline ball. McCartan rounded off the afternoon to send Down into their second All-Ireland final on a 1-12 to 0-9 scoreline.

The near hysteria which had greeted Down's first All-Ireland was repeated in 1961, with a crowd of 5,000 turning up in Newcastle to see them beat Dublin in a challenge match, while 6,000 spectators watched them defeat Meath in Newry.

Offaly were in their first All-Ireland final, and the interest in the game among their supporters reflected that on show in Down. As a result, ticket fever reached astonishing levels. Eventually 90,556 people filled Croke Park on 24 September 1961, the largest crowd ever to attend a sporting fixture in

Return of the glory boys: the Down team that successfully defended their All-Ireland title by beating Offaly in 1961

Ireland, and a record unlikely to be broken. It is something that Paddy Doherty is very proud of.

'There are two things that they can't take away from us. We were the first team to bring the All-Ireland over the border and we brought the largest crowd ever to Croke Park. That will never be equalled.'

Twelve seconds after the throw-in, red and black flags saluted Down's opening point from Paddy Doherty. Suddenly there was an eruption of green, white and gold: Brian Morgan hit a wide for Down and Offaly roared upfield to take a shock lead when Mick Casey's harmless looking lob dropped into the net. Har Donnelly scored Offaly's first point; then, sixty seconds after that, Donnelly sent a seemingly safe ball into the square, but Peter Daly snuck in and forced it past Eamonn McKay. Down were shell-shocked, but Sean O'Neill steadied them with a free.

With the trauma of their opponents' seven-point blast behind them, Down launched a scoring blitz of their own. First Doherty found McCartan with his back to goal, but the latter swivelled in the air and, on landing, thumped to the Kerry net. Doherty then repeated his provider role and passed to Sean O'Neill, who goaled. Tom Cullen and Tony Hadden shared points before Har Donnelly brought Offaly level from a free a minute before half-time. However, Down weren't finished: P.J. McElroy rose to palm the ball to Brian Morgan, who cracked a left foot drive into the net right on the whistle for Down's third goal, giving them a 3-3 to 2-3 lead at the break.

Without that scoring burst, says Paddy Doherty, Down's chances were gone.

'We knew it wasn't going to be easy because Offaly were every bit as good as us in 1960, but we just had a bit of luck. Offaly were two goals ahead with about ten minutes to go until half-time and we were struggling. I moved back to be a third midfielder and the first one I lobbed in, James scored. The second one I lobbed in, Sean O'Neill put it in the net and, on the third one, P.J. broke the ball to Brian Morgan and Brian put it in the net. If we hadn't scored those three goals Offaly would have beaten us.'

McCartan pointed a free to open the second half scoring, then four points were shared by Donnelly (who kicked two frees), Doherty and Jarlath Carey. Donnelly kicked another free, and Down missed some chances before Sean Brererton brought his team to within just two points a minute from time. Donnelly tightened the margin with a free, but Offaly's time was up and Down were All-Ireland champions again, 3-6 to 2-8.

For the second consecutive year, Croke Park was taken over by jubilant Down followers, and forty gardai were needed to get captain Paddy Doherty to the Hogan Stand to receive the Cup. Doherty hadn't been captain at the start of the year, but he assumed responsibility when Kevin Mussen lost his place for the All-Ireland semi-final.

Leading Down out on All-Ireland day, and being the man entrusted with lifting the Sam Maguire, made 1961 particularly special for Doherty, even if he wasn't too enamoured with another aspect of the winning captain's role.

Watched by his team-mates, Paddy Doherty raises Gaelic football's holy grail aloft at GAA headquarters for the second year in succession

'It was great to be captain, but I didn't like the speeches. I think I made the shortest speech in history. I said, "Thanks, Offaly", and away I went.'

Doherty also fulfilled an ambition that he never thought he would when his team won their second All-Ireland.

'I remember being down in Kerry and talking to Bob Stack, who had six All-Irelands. I told him that I would be satisfied if I got one. But he said, "If you get one, you look for more", and he was right.'

Down's 1961 All-Ireland winning team was:

DOWN 1961		
	Eamonn McKay	
George Lavery	Leo Murphy	Pat Rice
Patsy O'Hagan	Dan McCartan	John Smith
Jarlath Carey		Joe Lennon
Sean O'Neill	James McCartan	Paddy Doherty
Tony Hadden	P.J. McElroy	Brian Morgan
Substitutes		
Kevin O'Neill for Rice; Rice for Lavery		

A county that hadn't even won an Ulster title just four years previously lapped up a second triumphal homecoming. The squad went on a sightseeing tour of Dublin on the Monday after the final, culminating in a visit to Kilmainham Gaol. Like the year before, the party crawled through Meath and Louth before arriving in an ecstatic Newry town, and weaving its way through to Newcastle. Before the team left Newry, manager Barney Carr led the huge crowd in a rendition of 'The Star of the County Down'.

Celebrations following the 1961 success weren't as extended as they had been the year before, and Down started 1962 well. They won the National League and embarked on a successful tour of the United States, winning matches in Boston, Chicago, Cleveland, Philadelphia and San Francisco.

The Ulster championship started well too, as Down eased past Fermanagh and Tyrone into a final meeting with Cavan. The Breffni squad's shock 3-6 to 0-5 win ended Down's two-year run of provincial success. That year remains the great 'one that might have been' for both Down and Paddy Doherty.

'We should have won the third year. That was the mistake we made: being beaten by Cavan in the Ulster final at Casement in 1962. That would have been the easy All-Ireland. Roscommon beat Cavan in the semi-final; then Kerry ate Roscommon in the final. We would have won because we had the best team.

'We were leading by two points against Cavan in Casement and George Lavery got hurt, and before we got a sub on, Jimmy Stafford had scored two goals. We really missed out because we were the best in 1962.'

Man of the Match: Sean O'Neill

Sean O'Neill having a thump at goal in the 1968 All-Ireland final

Down enjoyed an encouraging McKenna Cup campaign in 1955. In their first round game they easily beat Antrim in a match that saw the introduction of two promising young players to the senior county team – James McCartan

and Joe Lennon. The Mourne squad was unlucky to lose their next match in the competition to Cavan by a point.

As well as reporting the loss to Cavan, the *Frontier Sentinel* newspaper carried a picture of the Abbey Christian Brothers school's under-14 team. Seated at the front, with the ball at his feet, was the junior team's captain – Sean O'Neill.

When discussions are held about who might be the best Gaelic footballer ever, a few names always pop up: Kerry's Mick O'Connell and Jack O'Shea; Galway's Sean Purcell; Cavan's John Joe O'Reilly; and Sean O'Neill. When the subject of best forward ever to have played the game comes up, there is seldom any discussion: it's inevitably Sean O'Neill.

O'Neill was selected in both the GAA's Centenary Year team and 'Team of the Millennium' at right half-forward, where he won All-Ireland medals in 1960 and 1961; but it was his revolutionising of the full-forward position that marks him as a truly exceptional player.

O'Neill brought his enormous repertoire of skills to the edge of the square, giving the full-back more to worry about than a big man who might fist the ball into the net and pick up the odd break. O'Neill's eye for goal was second to one, and his scores came at crucial times, like his brilliant, opportunist effort against Kerry in the 1968 All-Ireland final. He formed one of Gaelic football's most devastating forward partnerships with Paddy Doherty. If one didn't score, he set up the other. But most of the time they just both scored.

O'Neill picked up All-Star awards in 1971 and 1972 – the first two years of the scheme – and also won a record eight Railway Cup medals with Ulster. He carried his success on to management and led Down to the All-Ireland minor title, Ulster to the Railway Cup and Queen's University to the Sigerson Cup.

5

The Sixth Sense

DOWN 1968

Joe Lennon jokingly referred to the protests that marked the unprecedented civic reception at Belfast City Hall for the team he had captained in the 1968 All-Ireland final as 'a right royal welcome'.

Belfast Lord Mayor William Geddes made the gesture in recognition of Down's third Sam Maguire win in less than a decade. However, councillor Eileen Paisley, who led the picket, and her fellow protesters didn't appreciate the welcome mat being laid out for a GAA team.

Tension between Catholics, Protestants and the Northern Ireland administration at Stormont had been steadily rising that year and, a week after the Down squad visited the City Hall, a civil rights march was broken up amid violent scenes in Derry. The North was on the cusp of a quarter of a century of 'Troubles', and the GAA, like the rest of society, felt the effects.

Down's 1968 victory, as well as completing their hat-trick of All-Irelands for the decade, also marked Ulster's sixth in twenty-five years. If, after that year, it had been asked which Ulster county would be most likely to win the All-Ireland next, the answer would almost inevitably have been Down. Nobody could have dreamed that it was to be a wait of nearly another twenty-five years before the Sam Maguire would again return north.

 Down was ever present on Ulster final day during the Sixties, winning provincial titles in 1963, 1965 and 1966, but they just couldn't progress past the semi-final stage of the All-Ireland championship.

In 1963 Dublin hammered them 2-11 to 0-7. Two years later they were beaten 0-10 to 0-7 by Galway; while, in 1966, they went down 0-9 to Cork's 2-12. The minors enjoyed slightly more success in '66, reaching the All-Ireland final before losing to Mayo. Six of that minor side would return to help Down lift their third senior title.

The new-look Down team got rave reviews in 1967, and many in the county – and the media – believed they could recapture the All-Ireland title. Paddy Doherty and the squad felt the same.

'There was Joe (Lennon), Sean (O'Neill), Dan (McCartan) and myself from the 1960 and 1961 teams. Colm McAlarney was coming through and he was a great player. Tom O'Hare was coming through as well. Tom was a good player. Peter Rooney was a good forward. Jim Milligan and McAlarney were really outstanding at midfield. We had a good team and we thought we would win the All-Ireland in 1967.'

The squad won their way through to their tenth consecutive Ulster final, but the All-Ireland champions-in-waiting were in for a rude awakening as Cavan cantered away in the second half and ran out winners by ten points, 2-12 to 0-8.

Hopes crushed on Ulster final day in Clones were raised a little when they put in a good performance to beat Kerry 2-7 to 0-5 in the *Gaelic Weekly* Tournament final at Croke Park in September. Down went into 1968, and the restructured National League, with renewed optimism. This was helped by convincing wins over Antrim and Louth, and a replay victory over All-Ireland champions Meath in Navan.

Victories against Dublin, Meath again, and Galway saw Down through to the league final where they beat Kildare 2-14 to 2-11 to lift their first national crown since 1963. It was the perfect start to the season, says Paddy Doherty.

'It was very important for us to do well in the league. People can say what they like about the league and the championship, but the National League is the second best competition to win and we were glad to win it.'

Doherty almost missed the league victory, and subsequent All-Ireland campaign, when he was banned from the GAA for a year. As a member of the St Vincent's club who were victorious over Garryowen in the 1967 London final, he was one of the Irish 'imports' whose eligibility to play was queried by the defeated side. St Vincent's responded to Garryowen's objections by lodging a counter-objection and, while Doherty was cleared, the London board, in March 1968, suspended the members and officials of both clubs after finding that the two teams had fielded ineligible players.

Consequently, Doherty missed Ulster's Railway Cup win over Leinster, but was reinstated, along with all the other innocent players involved in the affair, by the GAA's central council on the recommendation of the Association's 'mercy committee' on Saturday, 14 April. He laced up his boots again the next day when he turned out in a charity exhibition game in Newry, in which Down's 1960 All-Ireland winners squared up against the 1968 squad. The sides finished level, 2-13 to 5-4, and Doherty went on to make his competitive return in the Mournemen's National League semi-final 2-10 to 1-8 victory over Galway.

Down's first Ulster championship engagement was just a fortnight after they had dispatched Kildare in the league final. The game against Derry was

The Down team that beat Cavan in the 1968 Ulster final

a bruising encounter and has gone down in Ulster football history as the 'Battle of Ballinascreen'.

Cavan's 1952 All-Ireland winning captain Mick Higgins refereed the game and came in for some criticism for allowing events to spiral out of control. It was obviously a bit of a scrap and the *Irish News* report called it an 'unsavoury, free-ridden game'. The headline, 'Down oust Derry in tough match', struck the right note of perspective on the weekend Robert Kennedy was buried and James Earl Ray, the man suspected of murdering Martin Luther King, was arrested in London.

Two Derry players found their way into Higgins' book in the opening ten minutes, and the first half spluttered along without threatening to burst into life or anything like it. Down led 0-5 to 0-4 at the end of a niggly first half. Six minutes after the break the bad feeling claimed its first victims when Down's John Murphy and Derry's Tommy Diamond were sent off.

Down had edged into a three-point lead when Derry goalkeeper Mickey Hasson lost control of the ball and Sean O'Neill pounced to punch a goal. Derry, who had managed to keep the game close, couldn't claw back the six points and Seamus Lagan's fisted goal three minutes from the end had no effect on the outcome. The result was somewhat overshadowed anyway by the free-for-all that had erupted just prior to Lagan's strike. When the dust had settled, Down's Ray McConville and Derry's Mickey Niblock joined Murphy and Diamond on the line.

Paddy Doherty remembers Danny Kelly's point-blank save from Sean O'Connell with twelve minutes left as the key factor in Down's 1-8 to 1-6 victory.

'It was a very rough match. Jim McKeever was managing Derry and they were geed up to beat us. The turning point of the game came when Sean O'Connell was going through and Tom O'Hare was coming flying behind him. Sean heard the footsteps and fired but Danny Kelly saved. That was the turning point and we went on, beat Donegal, then beat Cavan by a bag-full in the final.'

As the biggest name in Ulster football, Down were obvious targets for 'special' attention and often found themselves on the receiving end of plenty of rough stuff. Paddy Doherty didn't mind too much: it just gave him more opportunities to punish the opposition with free kicks.

'Armagh were rough with us in 1961, there was the "Battle of Ballinascreen", and Donegal were a tough crowd too in the match after that, the 1968 semi-final. We just got on with it in our own way. We were determined and we just played football. My best response to someone who was trying to get rough with me and foul me was to score my frees.'

It wasn't just in Ulster that Down were subjected to rough treatment: their unsuccessful semi-final encounter with Dublin in 1963 was pock-marked by countless frees. While Dublin was the better team, and Down were no angels themselves, the Dubs' robust approach drew widespread criticism. Paddy Doherty's reaction at the time was scathing.

'It is all right for persons controlling the Association sitting in the comfort and safety of the stands. If they were out in the middle of the field I'm sure some of them would demand danger money.

'We were a beaten team when Dublin reduced this game to a disgraceful dockside brawl. For any player to kick another player lying injured on the ground is unforgivable. It is outrageous to think that legislators who see these disgraceful incidents do nothing about it ... It's a game of sport and should be treated as such. Primitive jungle tactics should not be tolerated under any circumstances.'

Donegal provided Down's 1968 Ulster semi-final opposition at Breffni Park. Doherty opened the scoring in the third minute and Down never fell behind. He added another point three minutes later but Donegal replied with their first score. It would be their last until just before the break, while Down reeled off six more. Sean O'Neill pointed, then Doherty scored two frees to stretch the lead. Dickie Murphy scored a point and Doherty added a free ten minutes before half-time. Two minutes later he scored another one. Donegal registered their second point on the half-time whistle to leave it 0-8 to 0-2 at the interval.

Donegal got the first two points of the second half and seemed to be coming back into it, but Mickey Cole got Down scoring again and Peter Rooney added another soon after. Donegal scored the next two points but, in the eighteenth minute of the second half, Donegal's challenge collapsed as Down scored 2-2 in the space of four minutes. First, O'Neill pushed his team ahead by six points. The Donegal kick-out went to Cole, who passed to O'Neill; Paddy Doherty received the ball and fired it to the net. From the next kick-out McAlarney won the ball and transferred it to Rooney, who fired it over.

Once again, Donegal's kick-out only started a scoring move for Down: Jim Milligan won the ball and found O'Neill, who passed to Rooney, who set up Mickey Cole for a second goal. Donegal managed two consolation points, but many in the crowd had already seen enough and departed the grounds to make their way home.

High fielding in the Down goalmouth during the 1968 Ulster final against Cavan in Casement Park

Down were met by familiar Ulster final foes Cavan in the Casement Park decider and took ample revenge for the hiding they got from the Breffni men a year before.

The reigning champions were first on the board and could have had a goal, but Danny Kelly's crossbar forced the shot over for a point. Mickey Cole equalised and Doherty pointed a free to nudge his team in front. Doherty and Charlie Gallagher exchanged frees, while a double helping of them from Sean O'Neill consolidated Down's position. Colm McAlarney got on the end of a move involving Jim Mulligan and Cole to kick the Mournemen four points clear. Cavan got the next two, but John Purdy's addition to the scoreboard gave Down the initiative again. Cavan pulled one closer just before half-time and Down went in leading by just two points, 0-7 to 0-5, despite controlling much of the game.

It seemed that Cavan would make Down pay for not taking their chances when two points just after the restart levelled matters, but Doherty regained the lead from play and his men never looked back. Doherty scored another free, then started a move that saw Purdy feed John Murphy, who pointed in the forty-second minute. Down's pressure brought about free kick opportunities for Doherty and he smacked over two more before Murphy added another point.

Cavan managed a point but Doherty continued the onslaught, scoring from play, hitting over a free, and combining the two when he knocked over the rebound after his free came back off the post. On the whistle, Charlie

The Down defence converges to snuff out a Galway attack during the 1968 All-Ireland semi-final

Gallagher managed a consolation goal for Cavan but it did nothing more than put a better look on the final score which read Down 0-16 Cavan 1-8.

The 1968 All-Ireland semi-final against Galway is rated as one of the best games of football ever seen at Croke Park. In an era when Down did more than most to entertain the paying public, their 2-10 to 2-8 win over the Connacht champions stands out. With a particularly impressive array of attacking talent on display, most of Down's games, particularly in Croke Park, gave the crowd unrivalled value for money – something Paddy Doherty feels has been lost.

'Supporters paid seven and six to get into All-Ireland finals then, and they got their money's worth from Down. Tyrone and Armagh will think it's great to win an All-Ireland, and they're right, but supporters aren't getting their money's worth. Tyrone supporters are delighted they won the All-Ireland (in 2003), but it wasn't an entertaining final. People will say it's all about winning, but with prices going up all the time we need to get better value for money.'

Down started brighter, although Galway almost opened the scoring with a goal after four minutes when Sean Cleary found himself in possession ten yards out in front of goal. The Down defence converged, but they gave away a free that John Keenan pointed. Keenan added another free shortly after, but Doherty pulled one back. From the ensuing kick-out Jim Milligan won the ball and transferred to Sean O'Neill, who set up Mickey Cole to kick it over.

Cole's next contribution was a cracker. Willie Doyle's 'fifty' fell short to Colm McAlarney, who found Cole dashing into space with an overhead pass. Cole took possession without breaking stride and thumped to the net. A Doherty free left Galway four behind, while O'Neill and Connacht man John Keenan's swapping of frees had Down departing the field 1-5 to 0-3 ahead at the break.

Three minutes into the second half Galway midfielder Jimmy Duggan lobbed in a hopeful ball from about seventy yards out that dropped towards Down goalkeeper Danny Kelly. Kelly caught the ball and cleared, but the umpires judged him over the line and Galway were awarded a goal. Another controversial incident followed soon after when Galway full-forward Mattie McDonagh won what appeared to be a soft penalty, Kelly again judged at fault. John Keenan stepped up to take it and, although Kelly redeemed himself by saving the kick, the ball stayed in play and Cyril Dunne managed to bundle it into the net.

Galway pushed forward, but couldn't kill off the game. Down pulled level, went ahead, and were pegged back in the ten minutes after the goal. Two Keenan frees pushed Galway into a two-point lead with the clock ticking away and Down needed a shot of inspiration to stay alive. Sean O'Neill provided it.

Peter Rooney capitalised on a mistimed Noel Tierney jump, collected the ball and headed goalward. The corner-forward drew the defensive cover before flicking the ball to the unmarked O'Neill, who gave Galway goalkeeper Johnny Geraghty no chance.

Jimmy Duggan equalised a minute later, but O'Neill pointed Down ahead from forty yards out. With four minutes left John Purdy doubled Down's advantage. There was still time for Cyril Dunne to lob a late free into the Down square, but Willie Doyle emerged from the scramble with the ball to keep the score at 2-10 to 2-8 and Down were in their third All-Ireland final. Again Kerry provided the opposition.

Unlike the 1960 Down squad, who'd had the pressure of landing their county's first Sam, the 1968 players faced the new challenge of becoming the only team to win their first three All-Ireland finals. Kerry hadn't lifted the title since 1962 and the six-year gap was looked on as a footballing lifetime in the county. The Kingdom would not countenance defeat, but their opponents from the Kingdom of Mourne were equally determined to bring the goods back home. The 71,294 spectators who crammed into Croke Park on 22 September saw the Ulster champions prove that the victories of 1960 and 1961 could be repeated with an almost completely different team.

Jim Milligan won the throw-in, kicked the ball to Sean O'Neill and the Newry man put Down into the lead that they would never lose with just thirteen seconds on the clock. Milligan collected a Joe Lennon free a minute later and punched over. Mick O'Connell got Kerry's first score from a free, but Down pushed ahead again when O'Neill showed his astonishing eye for goal in the sixth minute. Peter Rooney picked up possession on the right wing

and headed for goal. Between the twenty-one and fourteen-yard lines he set himself to kick over the bar. The ball sailed over O'Neill's head en route to the posts but the full-forward decided it might be worth following it in as 'you never know when the unexpected may happen'. He was rewarded when the ball cannoned off the post above the crossbar and came back towards him. O'Neill stabbed his foot at the ricocheting ball and guided it past Johnny Culloty and over the Kerry line.

Down continued their burst of scoring and, sixty seconds after Doherty pointed a fourteen-yard free, John Murphy sent a low lob towards the Kerry goal that Culloty seemed to have covered. Yet again, however, O'Neill's presence of mind paid off when he nipped in front of the keeper and broke the ball back to Murphy, who fired to the net. The Ulster team had amassed an eight-point lead in as many minutes.

Kerry shook themselves and finally hit home again in the tenth minute when Mick O'Dwyer won and scored a free. Pat Griffin bagged the Kingdom's third point and two minutes later O'Dwyer added another a free. Culloty also did his best to keep his colleagues in the game by saving goal-bound efforts from Doherty and Rooney.

Brendan Lynch and Paddy Doherty swapped scores before Tom O'Hare, who had moved from corner-back to centre-back, boomed over a 'fifty' four minutes from the break. A minute later Doherty fisted over a point and O'Hare fired over another 'fifty' just before half-time to send Down off the field 2-7 to 0-5 in front.

Down were in the best half-time position of their first three All-Ireland finals but, as Doherty recalls, full-back Dan McCartan wasn't going to let complacency set in.

'Sean O'Neill got a great goal at the start when he followed through and scored after the ball came off the post. We played well in the first half and were leading by eight points at half-time. I remember Dan McCartan came over and told me to go to (manager) Gerry Brown to tell him: "Don't be bumming and blowing and praising them for the way they played because they'll go out in the second half and play nothing."'

Tom O'Hare was taking the 'fifties' because the regular long-range free taker, Joe Lennon, had pulled a thigh muscle in the first half. Whatever the psychological blow of taking off the team captain, it was clear that greater damage would be done if he had been allowed to continue.

Kerry started the second half brightly, but Mick O'Dwyer missed their first chance when he fisted wide. Sean O'Neill proved more accurate from the hand when he fisted over the first score of the half. A minute later O'Dwyer scored a free, then repeated the dose after sixty seconds. Doherty increased his tally but Mick O'Connell and O'Dwyer missed chances for Kerry before Brendan Lynch scored a free.

O'Neill and Doherty switched positions, but Kerry kept coming at Down. Pat Griffin pointed to narrow the lead to six and O'Connell followed with a long-range point after fifty-five minutes. Kerry were gaining confidence and, twelve minutes from time, Griffin pointed to bring the difference between the teams to just four. Down needed a score to relieve the pressure and Peter Rooney obliged by kicking over. Doherty, who had provided the first pass that gave Rooney his chance, kicked over a free to ease Down out to a five point lead with five minutes left. Mick O'Connell moved in to full-forward to try to get the goal Kerry needed, but another point from Rooney made it safe for the Mourne players.

Kerry completed the scoring with a point from D.J. Crowley and a consolation goal from Lynch, whose fourteen-metre free cannoned into the Down net off Brendan Sloan. With the scoreboard reading 2-12 to 1-13 in the Ulstermen's favour, Mick Loftus sounded the final whistle and, for the third time in a decade, the Croke Park pitch played host to a red and black invasion. Obviously keen to spare Joe Lennon's injured thigh any more strain, the Down supporters carried their captain to the Hogan Stand shoulder high. Lennon made it up the steps to follow Kevin Mussen and Paddy Doherty into Down legend.

Doherty is happy to hand out the laurels for that final performance to those around him.

*Forward John
Murphy scoring
Down's second goal*

*Joe Lennon
holds the Sam
Maguire up to
the delight of the
red and black
fans*

'On that day, Tom O'Hare at the back, Colm McAlarney and Jim Milligan in the middle of the field, and Sean O'Neill at full-forward really stood out. Peter Rooney played well that day at corner-forward. I was near my tether's length then.'

Despite approaching the end of his career, Doherty was still, along with Sean O'Neill, the focus of Down's attack. The bricklayer from Ballykinlar and the solicitor from Newry complemented each other perfectly, and the partnership they formed was one of the greatest in the history of the game.

'No matter where I kicked the ball, Sean was there to gather it and he could usually put it over the bar – or in the net. But if Sean was bottled up, he always knew he could hold up the ball and wait for me so he could give it to me. I was difficult to block because I could kick the ball over my shoulder and I could get the ball over the bar. We played well together.'

That wasn't to say that opposition defences only had O'Neill and Doherty to worry about. By 1968 a new generation of attacking stars like Peter Rooney and Mickey Cole had cemented their places in the Down forward line, while the Mourne county's All-Ireland winning teams at the start of the decade could boast forwards of the calibre of Brian 'Breen' Morgan and 'King' James McCartan.

'The one thing about our team in the 1960s is that any one of our six forwards could win a match. If one of us had a bad day another could step up and do it for us. We always had eighteen good players, a full strong panel of players. Kevin O'Neill didn't get on all the time, neither did Pat Rice, and they were good players. We had a lot of good players.'

Down's triumphant 1968 All-Ireland winning side was:

DOWN 1968

	Danny Kelly	
Brendan Sloan	Dan McCartan	Tom O'Hare
Ray McConville	Willie Doyle	Joe Lennon
Jim Milligan		Colm McAlarney
Mickey Cole	Paddy Doherty	John Murphy
Peter Rooney	Sean O'Neill	John Purdy

Substitutes
Larry Powell for Joe Lennon; George Glynn for Larry Powell

Ray McConville, Colm McAlarney and Peter Rooney display the additions to Down's trophy cabinet in 1968

The trip home with Sam took in the usual stops. At Gormanston College a guard of honour and a trumpet fanfare welcomed their teacher Joe Lennon. Civic receptions again greeted the team in Drogheda and Dundalk, while the crowds in Newry were, as Sean O'Neill put it, 'almost frightening'. The party arrived at the Slieve Donard Hotel in Newcastle at 3am on Tuesday morning, a mere five hours behind schedule.

Doherty, O'Neill, Lennon and Dan McCartan each won their third All-Ireland medal that day. The rest of the team seemed ready to build their own tradition of dominance. Six of the team were only twenty years-of-age: Brendan Sloan, Ray McConville, Colm McAlarney, Mickey Cole, John Murphy and John Purdy. Peter Rooney was a month short of his nineteenth birthday. Paddy Doherty and his fellow veterans were glad to see the younger men experience what they first had eight years before.

'The four of us wanted to win it for the younger fellas. It was three for us, but it was their first. Saying that, you never want to lose an All-Ireland when you get to the final.'

And it shouldn't have been the younger fellas' only All-Ireland, insists Doherty.

'We should have been fit to win another All-Ireland. Who would have thought Colm McAlarney would have only won one All-Ireland? The young

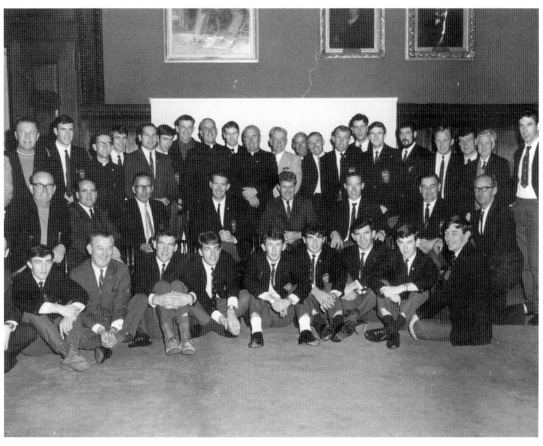

Down's 1968 All-Ireland champions on tour in Philadelphia

fellas won it and just didn't keep their feet on the ground. We had the team to win at least one more.'

Down secretary T.P. Morgan was aware of the need to keep the younger squad members' feet on the ground and his address to the 1969 Down Convention would prove prophetic.

'Included in the present team are a number of young players who have gained more honours in one year than other players have achieved in long playing careers. Therein lies the danger, as this might result in a sense of anti-climax, and cause a lessening of effort in 1969, and such an attitude would be disastrous to the team's prospects in the coming year.'

While the 1968 team may not have fulfilled its potential, Doherty is adamant that the teams he played on in 1960 and 1961 stand alongside the very best that Gaelic football has ever seen.

'We had the best All-Ireland winning team until Kerry came along with Mick O'Dwyer as manager in the 1970s and '80s. Before we came through Galway had a good team that won three (1964-'66). I remember talking to (Offaly's) Paddy McCormack after they had beaten Kerry to win their first All-Ireland in 1971 and he told me, "Doherty, you knocked us back ten years." Offaly were a good team and there was never much between us when we played them.'

Less than three weeks after their All-Ireland success Down set off for America in a bid to regain their 'World Championship' crown. The team lost the first leg of the final to New York by a point, 1-9 to 1-8, in Gaelic Park. The second leg, which was also held at the Bronx venue, saw Down overturn their one-point deficit to win, 2-11 to 1-9. They finished as 'World Champions' on an aggregate score of 3-19 to 2-18.

Just two days after arriving back in Ireland, the still jet-lagged world champions lost by a point, 1-11 to 2-7, to a touring party of Australian Rules footballers.

More familiar opposition was disposed of the following year, and Down secured their fourteenth Ulster final appearance in a row, but Cavan were too good and won 2-13 to 2-6. The next year, 1970, was the first without Down in the Ulster decider since 1957. They wouldn't appear in another All-Ireland final for more than twenty years. When they did get there, in 1991, they maintained the county's proud tradition of never losing a final. They did the same in 1994.

Like the teams of the 1960s, the '91 and '94 teams knew how to win in Croke Park when it mattered most. The special 'sixth sense' that comes with the famous red and black jersey had been created by the teams that Paddy Doherty played on in 1960, '61 and '68.

'Once we got to Croke Park it was a different kettle of fish. Down played their best football in Croke Park. We still do. We have been in five All-Ireland finals and won them all. Kerry have never beaten us in an All-Ireland semi-final or final. Down teams know the tradition and what the teams before them have done. Once they get to the final they don't want to break the link. God help the Down captain that gets to an All-Ireland final and loses it.'

Man of the Match: Joe Lennon

It may be said that Joe Lennon has made a greater impact on Gaelic football than any player before or since. It wasn't for anything he did on the pitch, although his curriculum vitae on that front is more impressive than most: three All-Ireland medals, including one as captain in 1968; three National League medals; seven Ulster championships and four Railway Cups.

However, it is for his work in coaching the skills of the game and codifying the rules that marks out his importance to the sport.

His first book, *Coaching Gaelic Football for Champions*, was published in 1963 and led to the founding of the first national Gaelic football coaching course at Gormanston College in Meath, where Lennon was a teacher. Further books and films followed, raising the coaching of the game to a new level and changing the perception of what it took to excel on the field.

His next project was to redraft and rewrite the rules of the game with new clarity. His research lasted fourteen years until, at a special congress in 1990, the GAA adopted Lennon's draft of the rules and definition of terms, such as 'hand-pass' and 'tackle', as the official code of the game.

Meanwhile, Lennon's impact while playing in the famous red and black

Joe Lennon

strip was hardly insignificant. His midfield partnership with Jarlath Carey was the foundation of Down's wins in 1960 and 1961, while his captaincy and experience from left half-back were crucial in 1968 – even though he only lasted for one half of that year's All-Ireland final.

After pulling a thigh muscle, Lennon proved himself a true leader by staying on the sideline for the second half, well aware of what was best for his team. He received his reward at the end of the afternoon when he collected the Sam Maguire.

6

'Back Where We Belong'

DOWN 1991, 1994

If any county was going to end Ulster's All-Ireland famine, it was always likely to be Down. At least, that's what Down people will tell you.

Between 1968 and 1991 only Armagh and Tyrone reached the final, Armagh losing to Dublin in 1977 and Tyrone surrendering an eight-point lead to Kerry in 1986. In the same period, Down won just three Ulster titles but lost their All-Ireland semi-finals to Galway, Dublin and Offaly. Despite the statistics, Mourne GAA folk never doubted they were among the aristocrats of the northern game. The years since their last Ulster title in 1994 have done little to change that opinion. It is founded on unshakeable confidence or if you prefer, and aren't from Down, arrogance.

For years, their All-Ireland victories in the '60s stood with Cavan's five as the only examples of Ulster excellence on the highest stage. Everyone who pulls on a pair of boots and the famous red and black jersey is placing themselves on a direct line from Sean O'Neill, Paddy Doherty, Joe Lennon and the other legendary figures who brought Down to the pinnacle of the sport. Living up to their illustrious past is a challenge relished by Down footballers, and the players that brought Sam back to the county in 1991 and 1994 rose to that challenge and carved their own niche in Ulster football history.

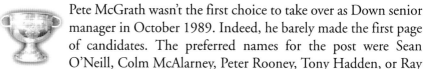 Pete McGrath wasn't the first choice to take over as Down senior manager in October 1989. Indeed, he barely made the first page of candidates. The preferred names for the post were Sean O'Neill, Colm McAlarney, Peter Rooney, Tony Hadden, or Ray Morgan. None were willing to take the job, and McGrath himself, manager of the county's victorious 1987 All-Ireland minor winning team, had to think about it before taking up the reins two weeks before the start of the National League.

Some players weren't sure if he was the right man for the job, and team captain Paddy O'Rourke contemplated retirement. McGrath called a meeting with the players to find out where they stood and convinced them he *was* the man for the job. In his first year he took them to the National Football League final, where they lost to Meath by two points. In his second he took them to the Promised Land.

While Down reached the final of the 1989-90 National Football League, the 1990-91 campaign did nothing to suggest Sam Maguire would be back in the Mournes before the end of the year. Indeed, it did little to suggest they would beat Armagh in the first round of the championship, and Down found themselves relegated to Division Two along with All-Ireland champions Cork.

Ross Carr sat out the NFL season, but returned to the county less than a month before that meeting with Armagh in Newry. He didn't find a team planning how it would win an All-Ireland.

'There was no real single-mindedness going into the championship in 1991. I didn't play in the National League. I only came back into training for the championship and, three or four weeks before the championship, there was a dozen training at most. People talk about plans that we must have made to win the All-Ireland back in October but, by the time the championship came around, we were only concerned about beating Armagh in Newry.'

They did, but it wasn't pretty. The conditions were terrible and Down only managed two scores in the first half. The fact that one was a Mickey Linden penalty goal meant they trailed by just two points, 0-6 to 1-1, at the break. In the second half, Armagh hit home just twice, while Down replied with six, but Linden's goal proved crucial as Down kept their line unbreached and finished unimpressive 1-7 to 0-8 winners.

'If, after that game,' remembers Carr, 'someone had said you would have an All-Ireland medal in six months, you would have definitely said, "That's a good lad, but he's not too wise."'

The Down team had played the Armagh game in brand new football boots, purchased with donations collected from benefactors by Carr, D.J. Kane and Liam Austin. At the end of training in Rostrevor in the lead-up to their Ulster semi-final clash with Derry, the trio were asked to explain themselves to the management and the county board.

'My first night back was five weeks before the championship and there was nine training. I said to Pete, "If you had told me this was the turnout I wouldn't have come near it." Pete said, "I know, that's why I didn't tell you."

'Most of us were in our mid to late twenties, while a few like Paddy (O'Rourke), Liam (Austin), and Greg (Blaney) were approaching the twilight of their careers. We knew something needed to be done so myself, D.J. and Liam identified five Down supporters and asked them for money to buy boots for the panel, and each had no trouble contributing.

'The county board at the time accused us of having a hidden agenda. I think they were aggrieved that we were trying to get stuff for ourselves, but it wasn't about getting playing gear. It was a way of lifting morale a bit.

Conor Deegan hand-passes out of trouble as Derry's Enda Gormley lurks nearby during the counties' Ulster championship clash in 1991

'Liam, D.J. and myself were hauled before the hierarchy. We were threatened with suspension but we were not for backing down. The board, typical of Down at the time, were pissed off that someone else was trying to do something. In the end it was resolved, and it was quite strange, because I think it ended up galvanising the squad.'

They needed that refreshed team spirit against Derry. Things had started well, probably better than expected, and the lads from Mourne led 0-9 to 0-4 after producing a sparking half of football. They had increased their lead with two more points when, ten minutes into the second half, Greg Blaney got his marching orders for a second bookable offence. Blaney was the one man the team could barely afford to lose.

'When Blaney went off we lost our shape,' states Carr. 'He was the cog on which everything turned. Greg would be the first to admit that he wasn't outstanding in every game we played, but he had an influence on every game we played.

'His greatest quality was that he never really left the centre half-forward position. Sometimes you have centre half-forwards going everywhere to get the ball, but he stayed around the "forty". It's so congested there, but he

Derry's Kieran McKeever can't stop James McCartan geeting his kick away in the first round of the 1991 Ulster championship

always seemed to have time and space. He was amazing to play alongside.'

Derry clawed the deficit back to three points with nine minutes left before Eamonn Burns volleyed a Brian McGilligan fist-pass home from the edge of the square to level the scores at 1-8 to 0-11. Joe Brolly pushed Derry into the lead and Enda Gormley seemed to have doubled the advantage soon after, but

Down captain Paddy O'Rourke goes full stretch to block a shot on goal from Derry's Damian Cassidy

Neil Collins reached above the crossbar to save a point. It would prove a crucial intervention. James McCartan equalised but Derry regained the lead when Burns collected a long ball out of defence, crossed to the other side of the field, shrugging off challenges, and finally threw an outrageous dummy before firing over a stunning point with the outside of his right foot.

Two minutes of injury time had expired when Barry Breen won a free fifty-five yards from the Derry goal. It was likely to be the last kick and Down's summer hung on it. Carr stepped up and stroked the ball straight over the bar with plenty to spare. In the years since, the free has taken on an almost mythical quality among Mourne county supporters, but for Carr it was just another kick.

'A lot has been made of it since, but that's because of the end result, not the actual kick. If Down hadn't won the All-Ireland that kick wouldn't have been mentioned. It was part of my job. It was Mickey Linden's job to be a match winner. It was Blaney's job to be a provider. Everybody had a job and it was mine to hit frees, along with Gary Mason.

'I'm not trying to undervalue the contribution, but it's not like you've never done it before. There was a moment in that game when Neil Collins stopped a point that would have put us two points down. I wouldn't like to try to stick it in the net from fifty-five yards.'

Derry shuffled their pack for the replay but, in doing so, says Carr, they dealt themselves out of the game.

'I think Derry panicked a wee bit. They took Damian Barton back to mark Greg Blaney when he really was their Greg Blaney, and to take him out of their centre half-forward position was utter madness. But thank God they did it.'

Down kept enough distance between themselves and Derry to ensure there were no injury-time frees needed. Carr finished with 0-9 and there was little doubt Down would book a final spot against Donegal. They had a four-point cushion when Derry substitute Gary Coleman hit the crossbar with four minutes left, but John Kelly collected the rebound and started a four-man move that finished with Derry goalkeeper Damian McCusker hauling down Greg Blaney to concede a penalty. Mickey Linden tapped over to finish the scoring 0-14 to 0-9 in Down's favour.

Donegal were reigning Ulster champions and most pundits' pick for the 1991 title, but Down blew them away, and they were delighted they did.

'We played some of our best football in those years in the first twenty minutes of that game. They were a good team, but nothing more than that and they arrived at Clones that day thinking they were going to run away with it.'

It was Down who ran away with it. Between the tenth and twenty-fifth minutes, they recorded 1-6 without reply, the goal coming when Mickey Linden capitalised on a collision in the Donegal defence to round goalkeeper Gary Walsh and crash home. By half-time they were seven ahead, 1-9 to 0-5, but McGrath did his best to keep his players' feet on the ground, reminding them how Down had lost the 1974 Ulster final to Donegal after being nine points to the good.

Down continued to dominate, but their attacks were ending in wides rather than scores, and Donegal dragged themselves to within four points. It could have been one had Neil Collins not saved well from Barry McGowan. Instead it was five when Barry Breen finished the move that began with Collins' save by firing over the bar.

Donegal were spent and Down cantered home, eventually running their lead up to eight points in a 1-15 to 0-10 victory.

Kerry were the opponents in the All-Ireland semi-final, a meeting dripping in nostalgia. The encounters in the '60s when Down won three All-Irelands were fondly remembered, as was the fact that the football aristocrats from the Kingdom had never beaten the Mournemen. That was all well and good, but the Down camp knew it was irrelevant.

'There was nothing we could really cling to apart from tradition,' says

Carr, 'and it's the media that latches on to stories like that. Down never played Kerry in the '70s and '80s when Kerry had a fantastic team. If they had that statistic probably wouldn't exist. Kerry were in transition at the time and they had some of my heroes playing, but they were moving to the end of their careers. They were not the Kerry of old.'

They certainly were not, but they were still Munster champions and were capable of ending Down's All-Ireland quest. Down's crossbar was tested twice in the first ten minutes, which also saw Greg Blaney hit the Kerry bar and Mickey Linden put a penalty wide. It was then that Peter Withnall made the first of two contributions that have entered Mourne football folklore.

Blaney hit a long free in to Linden, who transferred to Withnall, who fired a left-footed shot past Charlie Nelligan. It was just as well that Withnall found the net as other Down forwards were struggling to get scores. At half-time they were a point behind, 1-3 to 0-7, but Kerry managed just one more point while Down kicked over six, and Withnall repeated his first half finishing. It was 1-6 to 0-8 in Down's favour when he took a chance on a long ball pumped in to Mickey Linden, who couldn't collect, and scored his second goal, this time with his right foot.

Down added three more points, including one from Withnall, who was stretchered from the field with a foot injury, and were 2-9 to 0-8 ahead when

Mickey Linden feels the pain after being felled for a penalty by Kerry goalkeeper Charlie Nelligan in the 1991 All-Ireland semi-final

Peter Withnall destroyed Kerry with two goals in the 1991 All-Ireland semi-final. Tom Spillane can't stop him this time

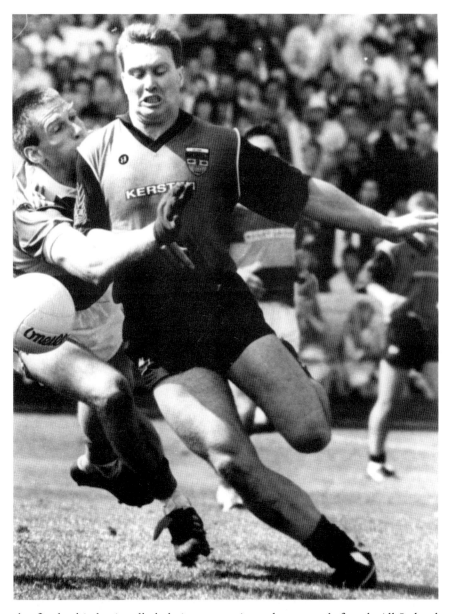

the final whistle signalled their passage into the county's fourth All-Ireland final.

They had, of course, won the previous three and it didn't take long for the players to be reminded of this. However, the winning tradition brought comfort rather than pressure to the 1991 squad.

'As opposed to having a monkey on your back we took the attitude that we're back where we belong. That year we were lucky that some of the '60s players came to training and told us what the day would be like. Unlike other Ulster teams, we knew what to expect and we were going to a place we were comfortable in. Our fellas were relaxed. The occasion wasn't going to get to them.'

The lead-up to the occasion was certainly getting to the county and Carr loved every minute of it.

'It was absolutely amazing. You would see kids at Mass, school, and walking about in Down jerseys. People came to watch you train. What would you rather do? Spend your career getting beaten in the championship or having to "put up" with adulation? It's an easy decision.'

Before they'd faced Armagh in the first round of the championship, no-one expected that Down would be in the All-Ireland final, least of all Ross Carr. Nevertheless, here they were and, with Meath in the other corner come final day, Carr took reassurance from the fact that the last time they'd taken on the Leinster side at Croke Park, there had been little between the teams.

'It only happened as we went through the championship. Meath beat us in the National League final in 1990 by a couple of points. We missed a lot of scores and they got a dubious enough penalty that Brian Stafford put away. As we progressed through 1991, and it looked like it was going to be ourselves and Meath, we had no fear of them. Had we not played them in 1990 we might have felt psychologically intimidated a little bit by this so-called unbeatable team.'

Meath's 'unbeatable' reputation had been forged in four astonishing Leinster championship encounters with Dublin. Their number seemed to be finally up when they trailed by three points with time running out in the sides' fourth meeting. Kevin Foley came to the rescue with a goal and David Beggy added a point from the kick-out to finally finish off the Dubs. The games had captured the imagination of the public, and particularly the media, who followed Meath's subsequent, less than impressive, campaign like awe-struck children. By the time they squared up to Down, few gave the Ulster champions a chance. When the counties took to the field on 15 September, Meath supporters painted the Canal End green and gold for the day, while Ross Carr and his team-mates were greeted by a Hill 16 solid with red and black.

'I remember going out onto the pitch, getting to the halfway line and looking up to see a wall of red and black. It was the most amazing sight I have ever seen. I remember walking around in the parade and saying to Eamonn Burns when we reached the Hill, "There is no way we are going to lose." It wasn't putting pressure on you, it carried you.'

Down took some time settling and didn't register a score from play for twenty minutes, but once they found their feet they started to lengthen their stride. The first score from play came from Eamonn Burns and put Down ahead for the first time. That they were still in the game was, according to Carr, thanks to Gary Mason.

'Gary Mason was one person who won us that All-Ireland final. Meath dominated the first ten or twelve minutes and they missed a few scores. After about twenty minutes, when Down hadn't been in the game, it was 0-4 to 0-4 and Gary Mason had hit three frees. They were all missable given the fact we hadn't played in an All-Ireland and the adrenaline was rushing and each free was against the run of play. Those frees kept us in it. After that we got a bit of confidence.'

With that confidence, Down pushed into a four-point lead, the scores coming from Burns, James McCartan and two Carr frees. Meath didn't score again in the half and Down went in 0-8 to 0-4 ahead.

While most supporters were delighted for the team to be going in four points up, it still wasn't good enough for Pete McGrath and he let his players know it. 'Pete laid it on the line at half-time,' says Carr. 'He was not a happy camper. He told us it was a very poor display and asked if we were just there for the day out.'

Down's response to their manager's team talk won them the game. Meath's Bernard Flynn got the first score of the second half, but his side didn't score again for ten minutes. During this time Down had registered 1-4. McCartan, Carr and Mickey Linden had scored from play when Peter Withnall collected the ball on the Cusack Stand side of the field. Four hand-passes later the ball was in the Meath net as Withnall found McCartan, who transferred to Blaney, who passed to Linden, who gave Barry Breen the opportunity to palm

Mickey Linden, one of the most feared forwards of his generation, shoots for goal during the 1991 All-Ireland semi-final against Kerry

the ball in from the edge of the square.

Three minutes after the goal Carr lined up a free fifty metres out when his captain told him the All-Ireland was Down's if the kick went over the bar. Carr obliged, although he disagrees with Paddy O'Rourke's assessment.

'I didn't think it would win us the match but I knew it was important because of the timing. It was like a Gary Mason free in the first half. The importance wasn't in the kick, but the timing.'

McCartan and Blaney added scores to push Down out to 1-14 with Meath stuck on 0-5. Down would add two more points, while the Leinster champions tacked on 1-9, inspired by the introduction of Colm O'Rourke. Still, Down had their chances and, while O'Rourke's entry to the fray knocked the Ulster champions back on their heels, it didn't stop them in their tracks.

'Colm O'Rourke definitely made a massive difference, but he had been on for five or ten minutes and Down were still going ahead. While Colm's presence lifted supporters and was important, it wasn't one-way traffic once he came on. We were missing chances.'

Down's best missed opportunity came when Linden found himself in front of goal with only Michael McQuillan to beat, but screwed his shot wide. That Liam Hayes had found the net for Meath less than a minute previously made it even worse. Hayes' score could have been Meath's second goal had Neil Collins not earlier made a point-blank save from Bernard Flynn.

Linden's missed chance was soon followed by a point from Gary Mason, which put Down 1-16 to 1-10 ahead with nine minutes left. Meath kept pushing and three points from Flynn and one from Brian Stafford narrowed the gap to two, but that was as good as it got.

Ninety seconds into injury-time, Paddy O'Rourke mopped up Meath's final attack on the right-hand side of the Down defence and found his touch deep in the Hogan Stand. With the final score at 1-16 to 1-14 Down were All-Ireland champions again. Proper order, thought Ross Carr, had been restored.

'I always felt it was destiny, that my career would have been unfulfilled if I hadn't have won. Players in other counties might feel that as well but, as a Down player, when you play for ten

Going, going, gone: Meath full-back Mick Lyons takes a trip over Peter Withnall's shoulders during the 1991 All-Ireland final

or twelve years, your career is unfulfilled if you don't win an All-Ireland medal because of the tradition and history. You just feel "I was meant to do this".'

The following men fulfilled their destinies on 15 September 1991:

DOWN 1991

		Neil Collins		
Brendan McKernan		Conor Deegan		Paul Higgins
John Kelly		Paddy O'Rourke		D.J. Kane
	Barry Breen		Eamonn Burns	
Ross Carr		Greg Blaney		Gary Mason
Mickey Linden		Peter Withnall		James McCartan

Substitutes
Liam Austin for Barry Breen; Ambrose Rodgers for Peter Withnall

Once the euphoria had died away, however, the reality of what they had achieved, and how hard they had worked to achieve it, began to kick in. A strange emotion took over, as Carr explains.

'I remember sitting there and thinking, "Fuck me, what do we do now?" It was strange. As the days went on it was an anti-climax in a way. The job had been done and there was no tomorrow to get up and do it all again. It was over. That's what it's like when you're on a mission for something. What do you do when the mission ends? We're a very simple, ignorant breed, Gaelic footballers. Your job is to play football and, when you don't have football to play, it's hard to know what to do at times.'

The euphoria returned when the team returned home, bringing with them for the first time in twenty-three years football's ultimate prize.

'Coming down into Newry is still unforgettable. Coming down the Dublin Road, turning on to Bridge Street and seeing the five-hundred-yard length of that street full of people. I will never ever forget it.'

 Down's achievement in winning the 1994 All-Ireland cannot be fully appreciated without looking at what went wrong after they lifted the 1991 title. The players deservedly enjoyed their victory – perhaps too much, says Carr.

'Having won it, the problem starts. The discipline in training wasn't the same. We rested on our laurels and got a bit too big for our boots. After all, we were All-Ireland champions.'

As champions, Down expected to be better served by the All-Stars selectors but, when the football team of the year was announced, only four Mourne players won plaudits. Carr, Conor Deegan, Barry Breen and Greg

Monaghan's Ray McCarron and Down's Barry Breen observe the minute's silence held before the 1994 Ulster semi-final, the day after the Loughinisland massacre

Blaney were honoured, but Down's haul was the joint lowest for an All-Ireland winning team in the history of the awards. Meath lifted six while Dublin, beaten in the first round, albeit after four games, won three. It was hardly the end of the world, but the blow to morale was the first of a number of upsets that took Down's collective eye off the ball.

A team holiday to Tenerife was organised, but there were disagreements with the county board over accommodation, spending money, and players' partners going on the trip. Then the players went on a tour of America over Easter and returned just six weeks before the championship.

When the Armagh game came around, Down found their form again, winning 1-12 to 0-9. However, the main talking point after the match wasn't the play but the physical approach of the teams, especially Down. It was, according to some observers, a 'vicious' game, a 'nasty' affair. It was certainly tough, but Carr feels it was singled out because of Down's participation.

'The game in Armagh was no more physical than any other in twenty years of Ulster football. It was the fact an All-Ireland winning team was playing. There were no Down players booked or sent off. The Ulster council read the riot act and, before the semi-final against Derry, we were told that there would be stricter measures against rough play. The week before, we had a meeting and were told that certain things would be clamped down on, but Derry just got on with it and weren't worrying about what the referee was going to do. By the time we got into it we were playing catch-up.'

The semi-final against Derry remains one of the most highly charged games of football ever played in the province. Derry had won the National League title by beating Tyrone in the final and both national trophies were on display before the 35,000 strong crowd packed into Casement Park on a spectacular June afternoon.

Derry approached the game like it was the All-Ireland final. It was an attitude that served them well at Casement Park, but left them vulnerable to Donegal in the subsequent Ulster final. They undoubtedly deserved to win, and fashioned their 0-15 to 0-12 victory from the free-taking excellence of Enda Gormley and a strong defence that kept Down's danger-men quiet.

With their All-Ireland title gone, Down supporters filing out of Casement probably imagined things would get better in 1993. They couldn't have been more wrong.

A new championship draw meant Down would face Derry again, this time in the first round. Instead of sunny Casement Park, the Marshes in Newry played host to the meeting on a sodden Sunday at the end of May. Instead of a tense three-point win for Derry, the visitors dished Down out their heaviest Ulster championship defeat since 1952.

At the final whistle the scoreboard read Down 0-9 to Derry 3-11, a twelve-point margin that, while a little flattering (Derry scored two late goals), painted a fairly accurate picture of proceedings. As it turned out, nobody could stop Derry in 1993, but that didn't mean a humbling loss at home would be tolerated.

'Derry had got to the stage where they were on a mission,' says Carr. 'They had learned an awful lot from the previous year and there was absolutely no way they were going to get beaten. We were annihilated on the scoreboard that day, but we contributed to our own downfall. We were relegated in the league, our training wasn't good and we weren't as fit as we should have been. I had probably my worst match for taking scores in a Down jersey that day.

I missed 1-4 in the first half.'

After the game Pete McGrath let rip. 'Our performance was a complete shambles,' he told the waiting media. 'I think Down fans are owed an apology by everyone connected with the team.' Carr agreed.

'He was quite entitled to say that. We had let the supporters down and we let ourselves down. We were in the comfort zone after 1991. You might think you're training hard, but it's not until you play against someone who has that total focus that you realise you are way off the pace.'

Some other players weren't so happy with McGrath's assessment and were particularly displeased with the fact he had let his feelings be known to the media.

'There were a few meetings where players weren't happy with what Pete had said. There was a lot of frustration about the panel. Two years ago we were All-Ireland champions, but since then we had been relegated and were hammered on our own pitch by Derry. Players were looking for someone to blame. It's all right getting beat, but getting beat in public is different. Sometimes it's not the fall from grace that hurts, it's the embarrassment of the fall.'

There were more rumblings of discontent when Greg Blaney and James McCartan pulled out of the panel. Down were unlikely to get very far without two of their most important performers but, by February 1994, both were back on board. Carr gives McGrath credit for their u-turn, with the naming of D.J. Kane – Blaney's cousin – as captain for the 1994 season.

'Pete made a very astute move naming D.J. as captain. He was the family link. Another captain would have had a difficult job getting Greg back. D.J. being in the family circle could bend the emotional ear. And once Greg came back, James was always going to come back.'

Another McGrath personnel decision brought the panel together and back to something approaching the level they had reached in 1991.

'Pete brought in Pat O'Hare, who has since passed away, to be the trainer and his enthusiasm was amazing. He was like a kid who had drank too much Coke. He was so passionate and just brilliant to be about. The training regime we went through that year was brutal. We had trained so hard we just couldn't lose. Unlike 1991, when the training only really started after beating Armagh, 1994 was planned out. We knew that to beat Derry, in Derry, we would have to be fitter than them. We had been caught in the comfort zone the previous two years and it was a massive task. It was a task that every individual member of the panel had to undertake. The response came against Derry.'

Down travelled to Celtic Park on 29 May and produced, with their hosts, as good a game of football as you could wish to see. Mickey Linden was the star of the first half, scoring five points, and his contribution helped Down go into the interval leading 0-10 to 0-8. It was high quality stuff and the Celtic Park crowd applauded the teams off at the break.

Points from Anthony Tohill and Eamonn Burns levelled matters before

Linden's sixth point regained the lead for Down. They were one up, 0-12 to 0-11, when Derry wing-back Fergal McCusker found himself on the end of a Joe Brolly pass and somehow hooked the ball into the net.

James McCartan got things back to a point with a brilliant individual score, but Anthony Tohill replied with eleven minutes left and Derry led 1-12 to 0-13. Down needed a goal and substitute Ciaran McCabe obliged, finishing a superb three-man move involving Greg Blaney and Mickey Linden, by hammering past Damian McCusker.

Gregory McCartan added an insurance point from a free to cap an astonishing victory in a truly historic Ulster game.

'Winning that game was special. Everything had set the day up. The weather, the crowd, the TV, that we couldn't wear our sponsors' jerseys. (Bank of Ireland had taken up sponsorship of the football championship, so Down were unable to wear shirts which had been sponsored by a rival bank.) It galvanised us, not that we needed it, and it was a great day to be involved in Down football. There was never any doubt after we beat Derry that we would win the All-Ireland. Whoever won that game was going to win the All-Ireland. The Monaghan game would just be another step on the way to that.'

Carr couldn't shake off the ankle injury he picked up in the Derry game. His place for the semi-final against Monaghan was taken by another of the stars of 1991 – Gary Mason from Loughinisland, a small village not far from Downpatrick, whose name would become known around the world on the day of the game for terrible reasons.

Around 10.20pm on Saturday 18 June, Ulster Volunteer Force gunmen burst into The Height's bar in the village and shot dead six Catholics as they watched the Republic of Ireland play Italy in the World Cup. One of the victims was eighty-seven years old. The next day Down gathered for a football match nobody really cared about any more. Carr wondered what the point was.

'I remember going to the match thinking, "What the fuck are we doing here?" There was a real emptiness. It was a case of get it done and get away.'

Down got the job done, finishing 0-14 to 0-8 winners, six of their points coming from Gary Mason. Carr watched from the sideline in disbelief.

'The mark of greatness doesn't show when things are going well. It's all about being great when things are against you. Gary Mason showed the mark of greatness not only to play, but also to put on the display of free taking he did, having come from home where his community had been destroyed. I don't know how he did it and I still can't believe it.'

Tyrone provided the opposition in the Ulster final and fancied their chances, but Down blew them away with a display on a par with their 1991 provincial decider hammering of Donegal. Carr and his team-mates took particular joy in that performance.

'Through the '80s Tyrone always felt they could intimidate Down, that Down was a bit of a soft touch. Before the 1991 All-Ireland final one Tyrone player was asked if he thought Down would win, and he just pointed to his

*Paul Higgins comes
away with the ball as
Monaghan's David
King tries to
intervene during the
1994 Ulster semi-
final*

chest and said, "No heart". But we knew we would win and it was good to beat them.'

Down started better, and Tyrone's attempts to impose themselves physically on their opponents just gave free-kick opportunities to Carr and Mason. After twenty-three minutes, Mickey Linden had the chance to find the net from a penalty, but he fired wide. Still, Down had enough in reserve to lead by 0-9 to 0-5 at half-time. Five minutes after the break Down were awarded another penalty when a bootless James McCartan was hauled down

Brian Burns gets to grips with Tyrone's Peter Canavan during the 1994 Ulster final

by the combined efforts of Plunkett Donaghy and Chris Lawn. This time, Carr stepped up and hammered home to make the score 1-10 to 0-5. Carr was glad to take his chance.

'The final wasn't going well for me and I needed that to kick-start it. By that stage I knew that, if I went home in the state I was in, I would probably have broken all the windows. I wanted to take the first one but, once we got the second one, there was no chance I wasn't going to hit it.'

Two frees from Peter Canavan and a palmed goal from Adrian Cush narrowed the deficit to three points, but Down responded by moving into another gear and finished 1-17 to 1-11 ahead at the end. Another Ulster title won, another step towards a fifth All-Ireland taken, and Cork weren't expected to stop Down's march – certainly not by Ross Carr, anyway.

'Before the game I really felt that we would win handy enough. Cork had a good midfield and decent defence, but they didn't really have a great forward line, apart from Colin Corkery.'

Conor Deegan leads the race to the ball in the 1994 All-Ireland semi-final against Cork

That was how it turned out. Down were 0-3 to 0-1 ahead after twelve minutes and doubled their lead in the next twelve with full-forward Aidan Farrell punching to the net after good work from Mickey Linden. Their opponents came back and Corkery picked off points to chip at Down's lead, but a Gary Mason effort lifted the siege and two points separated the sides at the break. Between the third and seventeenth minutes of the second half, Down broke Cork's challenge with six unanswered points. Cork went scoreless for thirty-three minutes, but Down had their own period of paucity when they failed to find the posts for the last eighteen minutes. Further Corkery frees helped Cork's cause, but Down were never in any real trouble and the 1-13 to 0-11 win was more comfortable than the margin suggests.

A week later Dublin beat Leitrim to complete the final line-up and ensure that Down was not the big story of the 1994 All-Ireland. While maintaining the county's unbeaten Sam Maguire record brought pressure from within Down, the media frenzy that surrounds the Dubs is incomparable in Irish

Aidan Farrell's goal helped steer Down past Cork in the 1994 All-Ireland semi-final. Here he shields the ball from Cork's Brian Corcoran

sport. After losing the 1992 final against Donegal and the 1993 semi-final to Derry, the expectation level in the capital was at a ridiculous level and Down were happy to let their opponents be the centre of attention.

'We were delighted Dublin got through. There was a fierce amount of pressure, hype and expectation surrounding them. That's great when things are going well, but it must be awful when they're not.'

The occasion couldn't have been more different to the 1991 final. The rain teemed down all afternoon, with the patrons on the uncovered, half-finished, new Cusack Stand particularly exposed to the elements. The teams shared the first four points of the game before, in the ninth minute, James McCartan found himself unmarked behind the Dublin full-back line under a dropping ball from Barry Breen. McCartan rose to flick the ball goalward, but Dublin keeper John O'Leary responded with a fine reflex save.

Greg Blaney balances on the Croke Park turf on his way past Dublin's Dermot Deasy during the 1994 All-Ireland final

Carr hit two frees, then Dublin pulled one back. McCartan tapped into the empty net in the seventeenth minute after Mickey Linden got behind the Dublin cover and gave him the simplest of chances.

The next six points were shared, with Jack Sheedy hitting the last of the half to leave the interval score at 1-8 to 0-7. Dublin could feel a little aggrieved that their superior possession wasn't reflected on the board, but Down's economy had kept them ahead.

'Dublin were all huff and puff, especially in the first half,' remembers Carr. 'They tended to need four or five attacks to get one score, while we would break up field and make the most of our chances. Our defence was awesome that day. The forwards did well in the first half, but it was our defence that saw us through.'

The four-point half-time lead had grown to a six-point advantage with Linden's forty-ninth minute point. A fifth All-Ireland looked secure, but Down didn't score again and had to withstand a fierce Dublin comeback. Charlie Redmond pointed two frees and Sean Cahill scored from play to leave a goal between the teams. Then, after sixty-three minutes, a long ball into the Down full-back line wasn't cleared and Dessie Farrell went down under defensive pressure to win a penalty.

Redmond stepped up to take the kick, under the Hill, keen to exorcise the ghosts of the 1992 All-Ireland final and his miss at the other end against Donegal. That day he fired high and wide; this day he kept his shot on target, but too close to Neil Collins. The Down goalkeeper parried the shot back to Redmond, but Redmond slid the rebound wide under pressure from D.J. Kane and Dublin's best chance was gone. Collins had made another timely, crucial intervention to go with his save against Bernard Flynn in 1991. Ross Carr appreciates the importance of the big Carryduff man.

'Neil Collins was an outstanding goalkeeper. He had massive presence, good kick-outs and was a great shot-stopper. I don't think there's been a goalkeeper who has had such a hand in winning two All-Irelands but doesn't have an All-Star.'

The day after the game Greg Blaney wrote in his *Irish News* column that, had the penalty gone in, the game would have been lost. Carr agrees.

'There is no doubt. We couldn't get the ball past our own half-back line, and James (McCartan) was coming back to help and win the ball, but was bringing his man with him. We were out on our feet.'

Dublin couldn't find the goal they needed and added just one more point as Down held on to finish 1-12 to 0-13 up and All-Ireland winners for the fifth time. D.J. Kane became the fourth Ulster captain in succession to lift Sam. His players could be satisfied that, with another job well done, they had proved that they were more than just a one-year wonder.

'Winning in 1994 was even more satisfying than '91 because of what had happened in the intervening years. It was the proof that we were no flash in the pan, a real "two finger" job to our critics – although the main people we were proving it to was ourselves.'

Down's All-Ireland winning team in 1994 was:

DOWN 1994		
	Neil Collins	
Michael Magill	Brian Burns	Paul Higgins
Eamonn Burns	Barry Breen	D.J. Kane
Gregory McCartan		Conor Deegan
Ross Carr	Greg Blaney	James McCartan
Mickey Linden	Aidan Farrell	Gary Mason
Substitute Gerard Colgan for Conor Deegan		

Donegal ended Down's championship interest at the first hurdle in 1995 and Tyrone beat them in the Ulster final the next season. For all of Down's achievement in winning two All-Irelands, Carr views those years, along with 1992 and 1993, as the ones that got away.

'Most of that squad would actually feel that they underachieved, rather than being lucky enough to win two, and I believe that. Time might soften that and, further down the line, we might look back and be happy to win two, but at this moment in time the feeling is, "Fuck! We should have had another one." A lot of

Mickey Linden

people try to be magnanimous about these things, but we fucked up a couple of years.'

That said, the memories of the years they *didn't* fuck up are special to Carr, particularly because of the special place they have in the hearts of Down people everywhere.

'It's something you always have. It's not something you think about every day, or week, or month, but it's part of a great time you were lucky to be a part of. One of the great things is meeting Down supporters, from their late teens to their seventies, and they tell me they watched the games again recently, and what they meant to them. It's nice to be told you changed people's lives, even if it was only for a day.'

Man of the Match:
Mickey Linden

For his length of service alone, Mickey Linden's inter-county career is worthy of note. The Mayobridge man played in Ulster championship finals in three decades and donned the famous red and black jersey in his teens, twenties, thirties and forties. His ability on the field, however, elevated him well above the status of journeyman footballer.

He was seventeen when he came into the Down panel in 1982, missing an Ulster medal by one year. He had to wait another nine years – the longest

Down had been between Ulster titles at that stage since their first success in 1959 – before he garnered a provincial award all his own. He seemed determined to end the wait himself, and was chief destroyer, scoring the only goal of the 1991 game that caused general mayhem in the Donegal back-line as Down cantered to the title. His scoring returns in the All-Ireland semi-final and final were relatively low by Linden standards, but his constant threat meant no defence could relax when he was around.

Three years later he stamped his name all over the championship, finishing the season with an All-Star – remarkably, the only time he was recognised – and as Footballer of the Year.

Beginning with their thrilling win over Derry in the first round of the Ulster championship, Linden tortured one defence after another, kicking point after point to help Down past Derry, Monaghan, Tyrone, Cork and eventually Dublin. His coolness under pressure when he presented James McCartan with the only goal of the final against Dublin epitomised his brilliant season. He finished the year with 0-17 – an exceptional total considering Linden wasn't a free taker.

Linden bowed out of inter-county football after appearing in his sixth Ulster final – Down's 2003 clash with Tyrone – in his fortieth year and third decade of play at the highest level.

7

The Fat Lady Sings

DONEGAL 1992

Donegal were leading Dublin by four points and cruising with a minute-and-a-half left of the 1992 National League quarter-final at Breffni Park. It was then that Dublin substitutes Vinny Murphy and Paul Clarke combined to pull back what seemed merely a consolation goal. Dublin launched another attack from the kick-out, and Murphy fired in their second goal to complete an amazing turnaround and give them a 3-6 to 1-10 win. Charlie Redmond couldn't resist gloating to Noel Hegarty.

'It's never over until the fat lady sings,' he said as he trotted past the Donegal defender.

'You could have shot me right there,' remembers Hegarty. 'It hurt me. I was very young at the time and I thought we were in the league semi-final. I wasn't even marking him. He didn't mean anything by it, but he's a Dub and they have to have a go at someone, I suppose.'

Five months later Hegarty watched as Redmond berated referee Tommy Sugrue for not awarding him a free as Dublin's time was running out in the All-Ireland final at Croke Park. Donegal had totally outplayed the raging-hot favourites and were leading by five points. Hegarty let Redmond finish before he had a word in his ear: 'The fat lady's singing now.'

 Things got worse for Donegal a week after their exit from the National League when Monaghan trounced them in Ballybay. With an Ulster championship opener against Cavan looming, all wasn't well in the camp. The problems stretched back to the previous summer, says Noel Hegarty, when Down demolished Donegal in the Ulster final.

'Donegal were beaten in the 1990 All-Ireland semi-final by Meath, and we had a strong team in 1991. Down really came from nowhere to get into the final and we went there expecting to beat them. We probably could have done a bit better that day, but James McCartan and Mickey Linden really destroyed us.

'In 1991 six or seven of the team were around the thirty mark and were thinking of hanging up the boots – more so at the start of 1992 when Dublin got the two late goals in the league. In the McKenna Cup, Monaghan beat us and that was the lowest ebb we were ever that. I'm not sure how things turned the corner.

'The beating by Dublin put us further back and then the beating by Monaghan made it even worse. At training the Tuesday night after the Monaghan game I remember James McHugh telling me that he wasn't going to come back. On the way home in the car he said he was definitely finished, but (Brian) McEniff managed to coax him into staying. He probably didn't let him sleep for a week with phone calls, trying to get him to stay on.'

There was still time for another jolt when Padraig Brogan left. Brogan, a former Mayo star, had joined the panel in 1991, but never made a particularly good impression on his new team-mates.

'I thought he was a very nice man, but he arrived in Donegal unannounced and wouldn't have been accepted by some of the older players. A month down the road he still didn't know people's names and some people didn't like that. I didn't mind too much because I was one of the younger players and I always had time for him. He was a good player, but was a very bad trainer so that didn't help either. His situation wasn't ideal.'

Brogan went back to Mayo, but he hadn't seen the last of Donegal.

The clash with Cavan in Breffni Park was a cracker from start to finish. The sides shared the first six points, Martin McHugh scoring two of Donegal's three and Fintan Cahill doing likewise for Cavan. In the twelfth minute Cahill added a goal to his total when he collected a Stephen King free that slipped through the grasp of full-back Paul Carr. Cahill drilled it to the net.

Martin McHugh responded for Donegal before Cavan goalkeeper Brendan McCormack denied Tony Boyle from close range. Cavan started to turn the screw, adding two more points to lead 1-6 to 0-4 after twenty-three minutes.

Carr, who was getting a torrid time from Cahill, was replaced by Donal Reid who went in at wing-back, with Noel Hegarty moving to corner-back and Matt Gallagher switching to full-back. The summer would see the switch become a masterstroke.

That afternoon, the move paid immediate dividends. A minute after coming on, Reid won a Walsh kick-out, then passed to McHugh, whose kick for a point fell short. Tony Boyle followed the ball in and swatted at it as it dropped towards McCormack, but both missed the ball and it dropped into the goal. Cavan protested – with more than good cause – for a square ball, or free out for a foul on McCormack, but referee Jim Curran gave neither and Donegal were back in the game.

Boyle and Barry Cunningham pulled Donegal level before the teams shared the next four points, leaving the half-time score 1-8 apiece.

Tommy Ryan and Ronan Carolan split four more points before Michael Fegan and Carolan kicked one each in the space of sixty seconds. Cavan led 1-12 to 1-10 with eighteen minutes left of play.

Points from Martin McHugh and Boyle pulled Donegal level before Carolan pushed his side ahead once more. Two minutes later Noel Hegarty finished a brilliant run out of defence with an equalising point, with Tony Boyle adding to it in the dying moments of normal time.

In injury-time Aidan Waters pumped a high ball in to the Donegal full-back line. It went over Gallagher and Damien O'Reilly and looked to be bouncing wide. As the ball hopped up, almost on the line, O'Reilly left his feet and launched a stunning volley over the bar.

While the crowd readied itself for a replay, Gary Walsh took the kick-out and Cavan conceded a free about sixty metres from their goal. It wasn't an easy chance, barely a chance at all, but Martin McHugh stepped up and boomed over an impeccable free kick. However, Damien O'Reilly wasn't finished and managed to fire over another unlikely equaliser. Finally, Curran blew his whistle to end proceedings on a breathless draw, 1-15 apiece.

Cavan had scored the last two equalisers of the game, but Hegarty knew that Donegal had dodged a bullet.

'We were very lucky to come out of Breffni that day. When Martin had his free, I remember saying to him, "Just make sure you put it dead" because we were level at that stage and I just wanted to get something out of the game. He kicked that, then they went up the field and Damien O'Reilly scored again. We were glad to hear the whistle.'

Whereas the first game was a thrill-a-minute dead even encounter played in beautiful sunshine, the replay was a dour, one-sided mismatch, played in rotten conditions. Despite Donegal's lucky escape in the first game, there was little doubt in the camp that they would be successful on home soil.

'At that time, Donegal were hardly beaten at Ballybofey so we were confident. Cavan definitely weren't. They were worried coming there and they never got out of the blocks.'

It started off tight enough and both sides were level at 0-2 each at one stage, but Cavan didn't manage another score for the rest of the half. Meanwhile Donegal racked up points from Declan Bonner, who hit three, Tommy Ryan and James McHugh, with two each, and one from Barry Cunningham. A Damien O'Reilly goal brought a little second half respite for Cavan, but it barely made a dent in Donegal's forward progress as they matched their first half tally of ten points and finished 0-20 to 1-6 winners.

Fermanagh provided the semi-final opposition for the second year in a row. Donegal managed to double their 1991 eight-point winning margin by recording a 2-17 to 0-7 victory, but the scoreboard didn't tell half the story.

Donegal lost the first half of the Omagh clash 0-7 to 0-6, but shut out their neighbours while scoring 2-11 of their own in the second half to record an impressive result without an impressive performance. The first thirty-five

minutes were especially bad. It took Donegal ten minutes to get on the scoreboard, Tommy Ryan finally obliging. Donegal kept with Fermanagh, but were mounting up wide after wide in a disjointed display. The game swung decisively in Donegal's favour a minute before the break when Fermanagh full-back Michael O'Brien was sent off for a high tackle on Bonner. Bonner converted the resultant free and the men from the hills went in trailing by a point.

In the second half Donegal moved into a three-point lead, albeit painfully and slowly. A goal was still the margin with fifteen minutes left – fifteen minutes during which Donegal cut lose and scored 2-7. Their goals were impressive enough: the first from James McHugh, the second a Tommy Ryan piledriver.

When the whistle went Donegal were in their fourth successive Ulster final but, as Noel Hegarty recalls, Martin McHugh wasn't happy.

'We went in after the game and everybody was delighted. Then McHugh stood up on the bench in the changing room and said it was a load of bollocks, that we hadn't trained, we weren't fit, we were just wasting our time and we would go to the Ulster final, get another beating and go home. After that the training became ferocious. There was at least a month between then and the final, and we trained hard for that month. We had a good foundation when we came to meet Derry.'

Derry were the talk of the country. They had beaten Tyrone in the National League final and dethroned All-Ireland champions Down in the Ulster semi-final. It was a role reversal from the previous year. This time Donegal were the underdogs and keen to do to Derry what Down did to them.

Donegal opened with the breeze at their backs and Martin McHugh got the scoring started with a free in the first minute. Enda Gormley equalised from a free a minute later before Donal Reid, overlapping on the right wing, gave Donegal the lead again. After Tony Boyle doubled the advantage, Anthony Tohill scored a free rewarded on the back of a foul on Johnny McGurk. Gormley and Dermot McNicholl points had given Derry their first lead of the game by the twenty-second minute when Donegal lost Boyle and Derry lost Tohill. Both left the field injured with Tohill lucky not to have been sent off. Boyle had taken a pass before being scythed down by Tohill, whose clumsy, dangerous swipe at Boyle damaged the Donegal man's knee while breaking two bones in the Derry midfielder's foot. James McHugh pointed the resulting free to level the scores at 0-4 each. Declan Bonner regained Donegal's advantage, but moments later things took a turn for the worse.

Dermott McNicholl took the ball up the right sideline and John Cunningham prepared to hit him with a shoulder charge, but completely missed the target and flew into the dug-out. No damage was done, but referee Jim Curran decided that Cunningham's action was worth a booking – his second of the game – and the Killybegs man was sent off to the amazement of the crowd.

Gormley kicked a free just before half-time to equalise, leaving Donegal to face a stiff breeze with just fourteen men. Things weren't looking good.

'It was a very rough half-time,' says Hegarty. 'We thought that Tony Boyle was going for a ball and was just taken out of it. We were annoyed about that. We were annoyed at John Cunningham's sending off as well. It was very, very harsh. He raised his elbow, but his man was away past him. There were a lot of very annoyed men, but it was easy to stir Donegal that day. It ended up being a good Ulster final for us. Donegal turned the corner that day.'

Damian Barton, who had come on for Tohill, kicked Derry ahead soon after the break. Tommy Ryan subsequently forced Donegal into a two-point lead when he won a free converted by James McHugh, then rounded Danny Quinn twice to leave the score 0-8 to 0-6 in Donegal's favour with twenty minutes to play. Ryan's performance, and that of centre half-back Martin Gavigan, stand out for Noel Hegarty.

'Tommy Ryan played terrible well and Martin Gavigan was out on his own at centre-half. It was tough and our men were getting it tough all over the field, but Martin Gavigan was giving plenty of it back to Derry.'

Derry managed to get the goal they didn't deserve when Seamus Downey toe-poked home after the ball had pin-balled around the Donegal goalmouth. Downey was standing in the square when he finished, but this square-ball

decision, unlike Tony Boyle's against Cavan, didn't go in Donegal's favour.

Derry couldn't press home their advantage because Donegal wouldn't let them. First, Gavigan careered through before being fouled for a free that Declan Bonner converted; then Gavigan won another free that Martin McHugh fired over from fifty metres. With sixteen minutes left Brian Murray gave Donegal a two-point lead, but two frees from Gormley pegged them back.

One of the consequences of Cunningham's sending-off was that Barry McGowan came on at corner-back. For the rest of the championship McGowan and Hegarty played unlike few corner-backs ever seen. Both attacked at every opportunity, leaving opposition corner-forwards bemused, shattered or both.

'We were both very fit and could go fifty or sixty yards down the field and run back and not be out of breath. Corner-forwards might try one tackle but that was it, they wouldn't chase you. Corner-forwards – forwards in general – didn't really tackle then. It put players on the back foot and, once you saw it work once, you tried it again. There was a danger that if it broke down you might be caught short, but James McHugh would always go back and cover for me without needing to be asked. That was very unselfish, very intelligent, but maybe he thought it would be easier to go back than try to get a pass off me.'

Points were swapped, but Enda Gormley's free proved to be Derry's last score and was immediately trumped by a stunning point from Martin McHugh.

Derry piled on the pressure, and both McNicholl and Seamus Downey

*Donegal captain
Anthony Molloy
outjumps Mayo's T.J.
Kilgallon in the All-
Ireland semi-final*

were denied goal chances by the swarming Donegal defence. Downey's shot was bundled out for a 'forty-five' and Gormley floated the ball into the square, but Brian Murray won it and headed out the field. He had taken two steps when Jim Curran ended the game with Donegal 0-14 to 1-9 in front and Ulster champions again. It was a fantastic second half from both sides and Donegal's performance was as good a half of Ulster final football as Clones, or anywhere else, had seen.

The Donegal supporters and players celebrated accordingly, although Noel Hegarty preferred things a bit more low key.

'I was young, just twenty-two at the time and it was new to me. I didn't like all the backslapping stuff; I would rather get into the dressing rooms quickly and watch from afar a bit. I would rather go in, have a sit down and think about it a bit than be out jumping in the middle of it all. I think it meant more to the people who had been there longer and had been beaten in a load of games. As I went on and got older, it started to mean a lot more.'

The Ulster celebrations died down relatively quickly and Donegal – team and county – turned their attentions to the All-Ireland semi-final against Mayo. For the first time Donegal would go into a semi-final as favourites. Their Ulster final performance had earned them that, despite the fact Donegal had never won a game at Croke Park.

Donegal took to the field on 16 August 1992, twenty years to the day since their first All-Ireland semi-final appearance, and served up one of their worst performances of the year. Luckily for them, Mayo did the same. It was a dreadful match.

Mayo already had two points before James McHugh initiated Donegal's scoring in the eighth minute. Shortly after, Joyce McMullan forced a good save from Gabriel Irwin and Bonner kicked over the resulting 'forty-five'. The game was scrappy and Donegal were clearly nervous, but they managed to take the lead for the first time when Bonner kicked over a free to make the score 0-4 to 0-3.

Martin Shovlin saved Gary Walsh when he swept up on the goal-line after the ball had broken away from the Donegal goalkeeper, and another attack saw Liam McHale fist against Walsh's crossbar, but flurries of excitement like those were rare. Numerous chances, including scoreable frees, were missed and Mayo drew level to 0-5 when Ray Dempsey scored after twenty-eight minutes. Both sides exchanged frees and went in with 0-6 each.

McHale opened the second half scoring after seven minutes and Donegal were starting to wobble. John Cunningham, who had lost his place after being sent off in the Ulster final, was in the dugout and knew what was needed. He made sure Brian McEniff heard him.

'Jesus Christ, get Manus on!' he shouted.

McEniff told Cunningham's Killybegs clubmate Manus Boyle to get ready. Joyce McMullan was withdrawn and Jarlath Jennings doubled Mayo's lead before Boyle got his first chance from a free, but he hit the post to record another placed ball miss for Donegal. He didn't miss again.

Tony Boyle ate into Mayo's score before Manus Boyle levelled matters on 0-8 each with a free. The game was there for the taking, then Mayo brought on Padraig Brogan. Noel Hegarty believes the switch went a long way to winning Donegal the game.

'At that stage we were in a rut and looked like were going to be beat. If Padraig Brogan hadn't come on we might have been. Other players took a lot more notice of it than me and definitely upped a gear, but seeing a man you trained with all year come on against you in an All-Ireland semi-final has an effect on everybody.'

With thirteen minutes left James McHugh was fouled and Manus Boyle kicked Donegal into the lead. Declan Bonner won and scored a crucial free. With five minutes left Boyle curled over a superb free from the left touchline, leaving the sides separated by a goal. Hegarty then unceremoniously stopped T.J. Kilgallon's forward run and Jarlath Jennings cut the lead to two. Tony Boyle settled Donegal nerves when he collected a Molloy punt, rounded Peter Ford and chipped over.

With injury time running out Boyle won possession again and rounded goalkeeper Irwin, who had stranded himself by following Boyle out to the Cusack Stand. Boyle fed substitute Barry Cunningham who was fouled as he bore down on goal. Martin McHugh tapped the penalty over the bar and Donegal were in their first All-Ireland final on a 0-13 to 0-9 scoreline.

Noel Hegarty – and the rest of the team – didn't get too carried away with their historic achievement.

'There were no great celebrations, we were just very glad to get over it. We were disappointed with our performance. We played terrible bad.'

A week later Dublin beat Clare, comfortably in the end, but not particularly impressively, and made sure Donegal would assume their old underdog role in Croke Park. The Donegal camp was delighted.

'Once it was Dublin we were playing, people in Donegal seemed to think we would beat them. The players and the management knew we could beat them, but the media didn't. I think Larry Tompkins was the only one who said we could win it. Other than that we didn't have a snowball's chance. We couldn't have wanted better. It would have been a different story if we had been playing Clare, but we knew we could beat Dublin. We were very, very confident.'

Brian McEniff was leaving nothing to chance. The semi-final had been a special atmosphere, but facing the Dubs in the final was a very different proposition. McEniff made sure his players would be ready, in every way.

'McEniff had a lot of stuff covered, from the crowds, making sure we knew what was on the clock, to the noise in Croke Park. Croke Park's a bowl and when you come out of the tunnel, if you're not ready for it your legs will go when the noise hits you. It was drummed into us so much, but on the day the legs were still very close to going. We watched the hurling final together and took note of the build-up and all the things that go on before it. We were well prepared.'

Brian Murray goes past Mayo's Anthony McGarry in the All-Ireland semi-final

McEniff also made sure each player knew all the ins and outs of their opponent on the day.

'He would name whoever you were marking and he was able to pick out a flaw in your direct opponent every time. He gave you confidence and could tell you what foot a fella kicked with, if he was good in the air, if he was brave, whatever. Even if a flaw wasn't there, he'd pick it out for you. I remember he used to say, "There's a hole in him" if a player was a bit cowardly. One day John Cunningham said to him, "These holes are fucking hard to find."'

Preparations for the seventy minutes of football were gathering pace too, with players going all-out to keep, or earn, their place for the final. It wasn't a time for the faint-hearted.

'At training we used to play a lot of twelve or thirteen-a-side matches and they were hell-for-leather. McEniff would referee them and a lot of nights he would have to blow them up because of the fights. They were ferocious and not an inch was given. Players were trying to get their places and, one night before the final, John Joe Doherty knocked Declan Bonner stone out.'

Hegarty's Naomh Columba clubmate Doherty hadn't played all championship after being out through injury and was pushing hard for a place in the first fifteen. On the morning of the final he won his place, after Martin Shovlin was ruled out with a neck injury picked up in training the week before.

'When we did runs around the field, it was always a race and John Joe

Martin Gavigan launched countless attacks from the centre half-back position for Donegal in 1992. He secures possession here in the All-Ireland final meeting with Dublin

was always in the top three, and he had come back late from injury. It was great for John Joe to get on, but it was terrible for Shov. It was a very honest thing for him to say he couldn't play. A lot of fellas might have chanced it.

'He had been there through the bad days and was as tight as you could get. In the runs round the field you would only pick second because Shov always won them. Then, nearly the last run before the final, Martin McHugh beat him – the only time he was ever beaten.'

On the morning of the final the Donegal team bus, complete with garda escort, headed for Croke Park.

'We had two police bikes in front and one behind, and all the traffic was stopped for us. Usually when you see that happening it's for a president or something. It was funny to look out and see people's faces as we went past. I'm sure they were wondering what in the name of God was going on. Then, seeing the Donegal people waving, with all the colours, was a great thing. You couldn't help but spot people you knew because the whole of Donegal was there.'

Apart from a solid blue Hill 16, Donegal colours took up most of Croke Park. It helped that both sets of minor supporters were also in Donegal's corner. Armagh fans waved their flags for their fellow Ulstermen, while Meath followers waved theirs for the team that wasn't Dublin. Outside Croke

Park, thirty-one counties were solidly behind Donegal.

When Anthony Molloy finally led the team out, it was just after 3pm on Sunday, 20 September. The next half hour was filled with the usual formalities that precede the All-Ireland final. Despite paying special attention during the hurling final, Noel Hegarty just wanted to get started.

'Everybody has their own way of dealing with it and I didn't really enjoy it. I was just keeping it blanked out. When I looked at the clock with a minute to go, that was the first time I had a look around the stadium. I just kept my head down and tried to concentrate until the match started.'

As the match got underway Donegal fans felt an awful sense of *déjà vu*. Martin McHugh kicked a free wide, evoking memories of the poor semi-final display against Mayo, before Charlie Redmond and Mick Galvin registered two points for Dublin. The Leinster men were playing well but, eight minutes in, Declan Bonner lobbed a free into the Dublin goalmouth which broke to James McHugh, who thumped it against John O'Leary's crossbar. James' brother Martin made sure the attack didn't go unrewarded and kicked over the rebound for Donegal's first point.

From the kick-out Dublin launched another attack and Dessie Farrell got a push from Noel Hegarty as he shot wide. Referee Tommy Sugrue stretched out his arms and awarded a penalty. Harsh, says Hegarty.

'Hand on heart, I don't think it was a penalty. The ball had been kicked and my left hand went out. It wasn't really a tackle. Dessie Farrell, who's a good friend of mine, would say it wasn't a penalty as well.'

Redmond took it, but scooped it high and wide of Gary Walsh's left-hand post. Donegal had enjoyed a let-off and they knew it. Noel Hegarty was more relieved than most.

'If that penalty had went in the back of the net, things weren't looking good for Donegal. I don't know what would have happened.'

Dublin were knocked back by the miss, but Vinny Murphy still managed to extend their lead when he collected a high ball from Jack Sheedy and kicked over. James McHugh finished a four-man move for Donegal's second score, but Sheedy replied with Dublin's fourth point.

Martin McHugh passed the left-footed free-taking responsibilities to Declan Bonner, who pointed from twenty-five metres, then Donegal launched a five-man manoeuvre that nearly produced one of the best goals ever seen in an All-Ireland final.

Martin Gavigan booted a long ball out of defence that was gathered by Declan Bonner, who offloaded to Anthony Molloy. Molloy took off down the right wing and launched a mammoth fist pass to Tony Boyle. Boyle beat Gerry Hargan and headed for goal, then palmed the ball across to Manus Boyle who, with John O'Leary beaten and the goal at his mercy, blazed against the bar and over from the edge of the square. Boyle's point levelled the scores, but Sheedy quickly kicked another point to reclaim the lead for Dublin. Martin McHugh equalised, but Bonner then kicked Donegal in front for the first time after twenty-two minutes.

Declan Bonner leaves Dublin's Paul Curran in his wake in the 1992 All-Ireland final

Donegal's James McHugh slips past Dublin's Eamonn Heery in the 1992 final

From there Donegal pushed on, starting at the back, where John Joe Doherty was fully justifying his late inclusion.

'John Joe would have got on any team in Ireland,' claims Hegarty. 'As bad as it was for Shov, you knew John Joe would do the job. When he came back in, it was like he had been playing the whole time. I remember in the final Dessie Farrell had won a few balls off me and it was John Joe, just in the team that morning, who put some fucks into me about it. I needed them, too.

'I think Dublin were waiting for someone to lift it somewhere, but it just didn't happen. Dublin could have had a penalty, but we could have been five or six points up. In a few minutes we seemed to go three points up.'

A Manus Boyle free and Tony Boyle point had given Donegal that three-point bounty and they held it to the break, with Dublin points from Farrell and Redmond negated by scores from Manus Boyle and Martin McHugh. Donegal went in 0-10 to 0-7 ahead. Dublin were stunned, but McEniff's preparations made sure Donegal wouldn't be.

'Before the game he said, "Don't be surprised if you're four or five points

Donal Reid played his last game for Donegal in the 1992 final. He shields the ball here from Dublin's Niall Guiden

Noel Hegarty and Dublin's Dessie Farrell jump for possession in a blistering final

up at any stage. If you are, don't sit and wait for them to come back at you."
That's what we did. We were in the driving seat, and it was just a matter of
get out and get back into them.'

Mick Galvin got the first score of the second half, but Manus Boyle
replied with another perfectly struck free. He won and scored another to swell
Donegal's lead before substitute Barry Cunningham was hauled down for
another free kick and another Boyle point. In only his second game of the
summer Boyle was well on his way to man of the match honours. Dublin
didn't know what was hitting them and couldn't do anything about it. With
fourteen minutes gone of the half Niall Guiden managed to steady them a
little with a point, but a Declan Bonner free restored Donegal's five-point
lead at 0-14 to 0-9.

Manus Boyle kept the points flowing and hooked over a spectacular score
to stretch his team's advantage to two goals. Paul Clarke kicked over a 'forty-
five' but it barely raised a cheer. Murphy kicked over a point to narrow the
gap to four and Eamonn Heery scored another, Dublin's third in as many
minutes, to leave them just a goal behind.

Tony Boyle left Gerry Hargan trailing again and won a free for Manus
Boyle to convert. Redmond chipped over a free from thirteen metres with five
minutes left. Manus Boyle completed his personal haul of 0-9 when he
collected above Mick Deegan and whizzed a shot low over the bar. Four
points separated the teams, but the Donegal players knew they had been
further ahead with less time left in the National League and managed to lose.

'That league quarter-final was in the back of our minds all the time,' says
Hegarty. 'We knew what could happen because it had happened before.
Vinny Murphy was winning a lot of ball in the air and we were worried every
time it came in high.'

Ghosts of Breffni Park seemed to stir when Murphy collected the ball
close to goal, but faced with a tight angle, the Dublin full-forward was closed
down by Walsh and his shot was beaten out for a 'forty-five' which Clarke
pointed.

Another Donegal attack finished in a wide. Joyce McMullan gathered
John O'Leary's kick-out and gave it to James McHugh. McHugh moved the
ball on to Declan Bonner, who cut inside and fired over Donegal's eighteenth
point. Less than a minute later Bonner was on the ground with the ball when
Tommy Sugrue called the game to a halt. Donegal were All-Ireland
champions and the only people in the crowd more surprised than the Dubs
were the Donegal supporters themselves. Noel Hegarty made sure he shook
hands with his marker and good friend Dessie Farrell before bedlam broke
out.

'Seeing all the supporters on the field was just amazing. The whole thing
was madness. Who in the world would ever of thought that Donegal would
win an All-Ireland?'

The team that brought Sam to the hills were:

DONEGAL 1992

Gary Walsh

Barry McGowan   Matt Gallagher   Noel Hegarty

Donal Reid   Martin Gavigan   John Joe Doherty

Anthony Molloy   Brian Murray

Joyce McMullan   Martin McHugh   James McHugh

Declan Bonner   Tony Boyle   Manus Boyle

Substitute
Barry Cunningham for Brian Murray

Hegarty and his team-mates struggled through the crowds to the steps of the Hogan Stand to see Anthony Molloy lift Sam and hear him proclaim, 'President of Ireland, President of *Cumann Luthchleas Gael*, clergy, and the people of Donegal: we've done it!'

The celebrations continued in the dressing room until news came through that shook the panel. The place was hushed when Joyce McMullan arrived in, wondering why the celebrations had stopped. The news was that Joyce's brother Gerard, who had been battling against leukaemia, had died that morning. Noel Hegarty sat, along with the rest of the team, not knowing what to do.

'From being a very happy dressing room with everybody jumping and champagne and everything, we were all sitting down wondering what to do. It was the saddest thing you ever seen. The bishop (Seamus Hegarty, Bishop of Raphoe and a native of Kilcar) was in, priests were in. Then a bit later, after a shower, we came out and we were told it wasn't true. It was better than winning it twice.'

It was Joyce's sister Maureen who finally confirmed that the rumour wasn't true, and McMullan and his team-mates got back to celebrating. For the Donegal supporters, the celebrations spilled into O'Connell Street, while a lucky five hundred fans made it into the team's victory banquet in the Grand Hotel in Malahide.

'There were thousands trying to get in, and Daniel O'Donnell was singing, and it was a good night, although I went to bed early enough. I remember speaking to Daniel O'Donnell, and that my mother was mortified because people were taking pictures of her with me. She was a quiet country woman and not used to that sort of thing.'

The next day the party set off for Donegal, first travelling from Dublin to Sligo by train, ensuring the inevitable tailbacks would only affect the

supporters. The players enjoyed the trip home, able to relax and move about on the train, although few got beyond the bar.

'We were all in the bar, but there was nobody drunk. Anyone falling about was falling because the train was moving, not because of the drink. It was good craic on the train and we sang all the way to Sligo.'

As the train moved through the midlands towards the northwest and home, other counties saluted Donegal's achievement. Hegarty was a little taken aback.

'We got to Carrick-on-Shannon and people had lit bonfires. We just thought if there were bonfires lit in Leitrim, what was it going to be like in Donegal? There wasn't supposed to be anybody in Sligo.'

In fact, ten thousand people were waiting for the team when they arrived in Sligo. The players got off the train and boarded a coach to take them into their home county. Just before 11pm the coach stopped and Anthony Molloy, Brian McEniff and Sam Maguire disembarked. The captain and manager then carried the famous trophy over the Bundrowse Bridge and into Donegal. McEniff carried Sam into his home town of Bundoran, where another massive reception greeted the team.

'Bundoran was bedlam,' remembers Hegarty, 'and when we saw the crowds there we knew the rest of the night was fucked and we were never getting home.'

In Ballyshannon there was a special welcome for Brian Murray, Gary Walsh and Sylvester Maguire. The same followed for Matt Gallagher in Ballintra. The tour rounded off in Donegal town, where thirty thousand people packed into the Diamond and serenaded the team with a rendition of 'Simply the Best'. It was close to six o'clock in the morning when Noel Hegarty finally got to bed. Hailing from Glencolmcille, he was still a day away from home.

'The next day we came from Donegal town and were in Mountcharles, Dunkineely, Killybegs, Kilcar, then home into Glen. There were massive crowds there and a big stage set up and everything painted. If anything stands out from that year it's bringing the Sam Maguire into my own club. Unreal times, just unreal.'

Man of the Match: Martin McHugh

In the prologue to their excellent book, *Sam's for the Hills: Donegal's All-Ireland Odyssey*, Donal Campbell and Damian Dowds tell a story involving Martin McHugh and Dublin's Keith Barr which occurred less than a minute into the 1992 All-Ireland final. McHugh had just sent a free wide and, as he returned to his position at centre half-forward, Barr suggested that the Donegal man 'didn't have the balls' to do the job. McHugh wasn't fazed and replied, 'We'll see who has the balls at the end of the match.'

The book also relates how McHugh scored ten points as a nineteen-year-old in the 1980 Donegal championship final to help his club Kilcar to their first county title for fifty-five years.

Martin McHugh

It's not difficult to see why McHugh is credited with a central role in Donegal's run to All-Ireland glory in 1992. He was the one who pulled the strings for Brian McEniff's side, the one who used the experience that came with a couple of Ulster titles in 1983 and 1990 – and the brilliant natural skill he possessed – to orchestrate his county's unlikely victory.

McHugh was at the heart of Donegal's superb second half against Derry – probably the best thirty-five minutes they played all year – and scored as good a point as the Ulster final has seen, hooked over his shoulder from a tight angle on the touchline.

In the All-Ireland final, too, he responded to Keith Barr's jibe in the best possible way, leading from the front to stop Dublin's best player dictating the game.

McHugh featured in another two championships for Donegal, but didn't play again after being stretchered off during the 1994 Ulster semi-final loss to Tyrone. In August of that year he applied for the vacant Donegal manager's position, but lost out to P.J. McGowan. Cavan snapped up his services instead and were rewarded when McHugh led them to the Ulster title – their first for twenty-eight years – in 1997.

8

'Pie in the Sky'

DERRY 1993

1992 was to be Derry's year and they knew it.

A National League final win over their neighbours and fierce rivals Tyrone was followed by a championship victory over the same team. The Ulster semi-final clash with All-Ireland champions Down was one of the most anticipated games in the province for as long as many people could remember. Derry deserved their victory and celebrated, but it was just an Ulster semi-final win. Equally, Derry deserved their loss against Donegal in the final and could only watch as their other neighbours took the path to the maiden All-Ireland win that Derry so coveted.

Twelve months after their trauma in Clones, Derry returned and again came head-to-head with Donegal. For the second time in just over a year Derry dethroned an All-Ireland champion team. This time, however, they weren't going to let the opportunity pass them by and, for the rest of the summer, they moved steadily towards their All-Ireland obsession.

 The Derry followers leaving St Tiernach's Park in Clones after the 1992 Ulster final couldn't believe their summer was over. The players, including corner-forward Enda Gormley, felt much the same.

'After winning the league, then beating Tyrone and Down in the championship, we were probably on too much of a high and I think we took our eye off the ball. In hindsight, our level of preparation for that Ulster final wouldn't have been the same as for the '93 Ulster final. It wasn't that we did anything different – it's just that, in hindsight, it wasn't as aggressive as in 1993.'

Donegal had succeeded Down in lifting the Sam Maguire and Derry were left to watch from the sidelines as the prize they craved so much went to their Ulster rivals. That, however, wasn't really the problem. It didn't matter if Sam was in Down, Donegal, Kerry or Meath. The problem was it wasn't in Derry.

'We weren't really worried about Ulster. We were worried about Derry. Our goal was to be the first Derry team to win the All-Ireland. I remember Joe Brolly came out with the line after the semi-final that we were seventy minutes from immortality. Maybe a bit strong, but there was some truth in it. Even if some other team came along and won five in a row, we would still be the first Derry team to win it.'

Derry went into the 1993 championship campaign with another defeat to Donegal fresh in the memory. They managed just a point in the second half of the counties' National League quarter-final and lost 0-10 to 2-3. To make matters worse, Kieran McKeever was sent off for breaking Tommy Ryan's jaw and was slapped with a two-month suspension. McKeever would miss Derry's championship opener against Down in Newry and, with Tony Scullion struggling with injury, Derry weren't fancied to make it out of the Marshes.

Damien Cassidy opened the scoring in the second minute and added another soon after. Ross Carr put away a free and Mickey Linden got past Tony Scullion to put a point on the board and balance things, but that was as good as it got for Down. Two minutes later Cassidy got his, and Derry's, third point.

When Conor Deegan couldn't gather possession, Damian Barton picked up the loose ball and found Dermot Heaney inside the Down cover. Heaney fired past Neil Collins for Derry's first goal. Down kept at it and Ross Carr kicked over their third point from a free to bring them within a goal of their adversaries.

Anthony Tohill then kicked a free and Barton added another to put Derry 1-5 to 0-3 ahead. Damien McCusker did well to save from Ross Carr and, soon after, Carr converted another free for Down's fourth point.

Before half-time Tohill and Gary Mason swapped points, and Derry went in at the interval ahead by 1-6 to 0-5.

Down came back at the start of the second half. Two points from Carr cut Derry's lead, but Down would be outscored 2-5 to 0-2 for the rest of the game.

'We had been at the door a couple of times,' says Gormley, 'and we were incredibly keen and hungry that day. Things went well, but there was a point halfway through the second half when they got it back to two points and kicked a couple of wides. I often wonder what would have happened if those had gone over. In the '94 match Fergal McCusker got a goal and we missed a few chances, and those could have changed that game. Both years, the results could have been different.'

Tohill continued to run the show for Derry and they were already six points ahead, 1-11 to 0-8, when Dermot Heaney headed for goal. He transferred to substitute Eamonn Burns, whose shot was well stopped by Collins. Unfortunately for Down, the rebound slid into the path of Richard Ferris who fired in Derry's second goal to put the match beyond doubt.

Burns managed to find the net himself in the sixty-eighth minute when

Dermot Heaney and Monaghan's Eugene McSherry battle for possession in the Ulster semi-final

he volleyed in from the edge of the square after Gormley's free had been fisted across the Down goalmouth. Most Down supporters were well on their way home when the final whistle called a halt with Derry 3-11 to 0-9 ahead.

After such an impressive display, Derry weren't expected to slip up in the semi-final against Monaghan, but for long periods of the match in Casement Park there was nothing between the sides.

After the first twenty minutes it had looked like Derry would run away with the game. Brian McGilligan fired over their fifth point after nineteen minutes to give them a four-point cushion, thanks in large part to Enda Gormley and Damien Cassidy.

Monaghan came back quickly and hit three points in as many minutes from Ray McCarron, Michael Slowey and Gerard Mone. By the twenty-seventh minute they had pulled level, but they had an escape when Cassidy wasted a good goal chance, blazing wide after being put through by Damian Barton. Gregory Flanagan put Monaghan into the lead, but Gormley replied a minute later to equalise. Ray McCarron pushed Monaghan ahead again on thirty-five minutes, but a Gormley free levelled the scores in added time and the sides went in sharing 0-8 each.

'It was level at half-time and I remember Eamonn Coleman being very sore on us in the dressing room. He introduced Joe Brolly and Brian McCormack, and those substitutions really made a massive difference to us in the second half. They got points and set up scores for other people and helped us a lot.'

Joe Brolly scored the first of his three points seconds after being brought on and, although Monaghan kept with Derry, their challenge started to fade as Brolly and McCormack changed things and Derry upped the pace.

Tohill and Karl Diamond scored points, and Derry were leading 0-12 to 0-9 and accelerating away. Eddie Murphy got Monaghan's last point to make it 0-14 to 0-11 after fifty-eight minutes, but Derry pushed on. Brolly's final point, and three from Gormley who ended the game with 0-7, finished Monaghan off as Derry completed a 0-19 to 0-11 win.

The demolition of Down apart, Derry were left to make preparations for the Ulster final fairly undisturbed by outside attention. Most interested eyes were on the other side of the draw where Armagh had turned an eight-point

Both sides agreed the 1993 Ulster final should never have been played. Derry made the best of atrocious conditions in Clones. One of their best players on the day, Damien Cassidy, shoots for goal as Martin Shovlin tries to stop him

Mark Crossan and Derry's Brian McGilligan tangle for possession in the Clones mud

deficit into a one-point win in the last eight minutes of their preliminary round replay with Fermanagh. They had also needed two games to get past Tyrone in the next round and were eventually beaten, after yet another replay, by Donegal in the semi-final. Derry kept their heads down and let other people get excited about all that.

'We weren't too worried about what was going on with other teams. At that stage we were obsessed with winning the All-Ireland. It wasn't that we felt we needed to do it; we had to do it.'

Donegal's defeat of Armagh meant Derry had a shot at revenge in the 1993 Ulster final. A game to match the previous year's thriller was anticipated. That game had been played in blinding sunshine; the 1993 final was played on a paddy field. Constant rain a day before the game had left the recently refurbished pitch in a shocking state. Enda Gormley recalls:

'I remember standing watching a club training session on the Friday night and there was a fella there, James O'Kane, who had come back from Australia for the match. He was so excited about it he had been down to see Clones during the week, and he told me on the Friday there's no way that the game

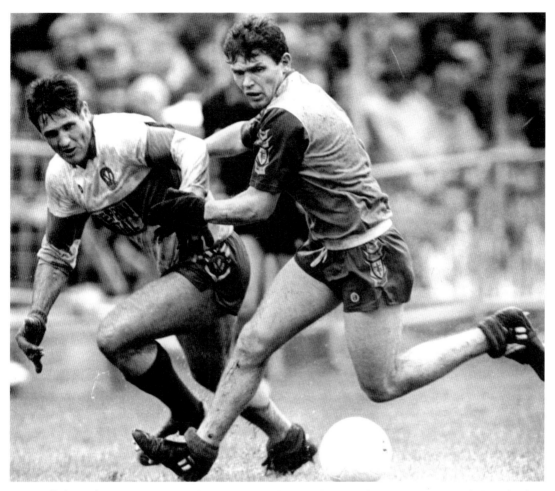

Matt Gallagher and Dermot McNicholl fight for the ball in Clones

was going to be played. I thought he was having me on. I didn't think a second thing about it.'

Once Gormley and his Derry team-mates arrived at the ground they were sure they wouldn't need to tog out. Despite the pitch being clearly unplayable, and conditions on the Clones hill becoming rapidly more dangerous for spectators, Derry and Tyrone played the minor final. It wasn't long before Derry's Cathal Scullion was lying in a pool of water with a broken leg.

'We arrived in the bus and pulled in behind the old changing rooms above the hill and, as we got out of the bus, we looked down at the minor match and, as they were running, we saw water splashing up. We looked at each other and the forwards were disgusted, but I remember Kieran McKeever and Johnny McGurk were delighted. It was manna from heaven for them, but it was more serious than that as well.

'There is no way that match should have been played; no one could question that. What happened to Cathal Scullion could have happened to any of us. Some of our supporters had been critical of our performance, but once they got on the pitch they all said, "God, we never realised it was this bad." People couldn't make it from one side of the pitch to the other without falling over. The surface was a joke.'

Considering the ridiculous conditions, both teams made a decent fist of creating a spectacle. Donegal started the game better and Joyce McMullan gave them a 0-2 to nothing lead from the kick-out after Manus Boyle had opened the scoring from a free. Another Boyle free gave Donegal 0-3 to 0-1 after nineteen minutes, Derry's score coming from Gormley.

Damien Cassidy pulled Derry level after half an hour, but Donegal finished the first session stronger and an excellent Martin McHugh point from a tight angle helped them into a 0-5 to 0-4 interval lead. The players trudged off, ankle deep in water, hopeful the clouds might give it a rest for the second half. They trudged back on for more of the same fifteen minutes later. Gormley wasn't enjoying things at all. Ten seconds after the throw-in Derry were awarded a free sixty yards from the Donegal goal.

'From a forward's point of view it's just disgusting playing in those conditions. You've no balance when you're shooting because your standing foot is slipping, and you can't control balls that are coming in to you. I had problems hitting free kicks from twenty-five yards, but Anthony Tohill hit a free over from at least sixty yards that was still rising when it went over the crossbar. That would be eighty yards in perfect conditions. I've never seen a kick like it in my life.'

After Tohill's free, Cassidy pushed Derry in front for the first time, and further points from Damian Barton and Gormley kept Donegal at bay. John Duffy finally managed a score for the Ulster and All-Ireland champions, but their crown was slipping and sliding across the Clones turf. Neither team managed another score and Manus Boyle got his marching orders for lashing out at Johnny McGurk near the end, as Derry aquaplaned to an 0-8 to 0-6 win. It was Donegal's turn to wonder at what had just happened. Getting beaten was bad enough; getting beaten like that was hard to swallow. Enda Gormley sympathises, but not too much.

'It was a terrible way to lose your All-Ireland title, in those conditions, but I'm still convinced we would have won on a good day as well. I've never been more convinced that we would win a match than I was before that one, and I would normally be a bit more worried. At the training session on the Wednesday before the Ulster final there wasn't a ball dropped and every man was totally tuned in. It was almost perfect focus.'

With an Ulster title in the bag, the focus switched to the All-Ireland semi-final meeting with Dublin. If Derry felt pressured to win an All-Ireland it was nothing compared to Dublin, who could still remember the beating they took from the unfancied Donegal in the final the year before. The Dubs managed some revenge by beating Donegal in the National League final replay, and again carried the hopes of the Hill into their clash with Derry. It was clear when semi-final day came around, however, that apart from the famous terrace, Derry supporters had filled Croke Park. They gave their heroes the appropriate welcome, something that Enda Gormley will never forget.

Derry's Fergal McCusker and Donegal's Paul Carr splash around in Clones

'There was a big Derry contingent in the Cusack Stand and we were heading straight for it when we came out. Running out for the semi-final, there was just a massive roar. I've never heard anything like it.'

Once they got on the pitch there was still time for the waiting photographers – as well as some team-mates – to feel annoyed at Joe Brolly.

'Brolly came up with the idea that if he didn't stand in for the photo nobody could rip it off, so he stayed out of it. The photographers noticed and weren't moving, so we had to come back in. We were only interested in getting warmed up and ready for the match, so there were a few choice words said to Brolly.'

Once the pictures had been taken and the match got started, Derry jumped out to a three-point lead before Charlie Redmond got Dublin on the board in the fourteenth minute. After that, Derry managed just one more point while Dublin racked up another eight. Jack Sheedy was orchestrating things for the Dubs, and points from Paul Bealin and Paul Curran stood out as they roared into the break 0-9 to 0-4 ahead.

Derry were more than a little shell-shocked as they made their way back to the changing room. As they did, one supporter let his feelings be loudly known.

Derry's Joe Brolly heads for goal in the 1993 All-Ireland semi-final

'I remember going off at half-time,' says Gormley, 'and as we were going down the tunnel between the Canal End and Hogan Stand one supporter shouted, "Typical fucking Derry team. They promise so much then go down to Croke Park and shit in the nest." We all heard it.'

In the safety of the changing room, trainer Mickey Moran – normally a quiet, laid back figure – took the floor and stung his players into action.

'Normally Eamonn Coleman was the vocal man in our changing room, but that day Mickey Moran took over and I've never seen him raised like it in my life. The surprise element of that shocked us and lifted us. He had also heard what the supporter said, and he used that as well.

'I had grown up watching Derry teams in the 1970s in two All-Ireland semi-finals and a National League final. The statement struck a chord with me because I was at those games and I remember the disgust coming home with my parents and my uncle.'

Derry came back onto the field resolved not to send the supporters, and themselves, home disappointed.

'We were lucky to get an early free and we got the gap back to three fairly quickly, but it went three-four, three-four a couple of times, but we could never get it down to two points. With about ten minutes to go we managed to get it down to two points and, as soon as we got that, we were on a roll.'

Shortly after the resumption Derry had the gap down to three, but Eamonn Heery pushed Dublin back out to four points a minute later and the sides swapped the next four scores. Gormley got Derry's next three points, while Charlie Redmond kicked one for Dublin to have the board read 0-13 to 0-11 with ten minutes left. From there Derry charged for the line. Brian McGilligan had come back into the game and set the tone for Derry's revival with an almighty shoulder charge on Jack Sheedy, after which the Dublin centre half-forward wasn't the same.

With seven minutes left, Gormley chipped over a thirteen-metre free – 'I very nearly missed it' – to level the proceedings. A minute later captain Henry Downey kicked his second point from centre half-back to give Derry a short-lived lead that Redmond wiped out with a free less than sixty seconds later.

It was then that Dermott McNicholl sent a hand-pass to Johnny McGurk, who was overlapping from wing-back. The pass was too high and took McGurk to a few yards inside the touchline under the Hogan Stand. No bother. McGurk sold a dummy on his right foot before sweeping over a stunning point from the thirteen-metre line. Enda Gormley watched from the other side of the field.

'I was confident in Johnny. He always played down his left foot, but if you knew him in club football you knew he scored nearly more points with his left after dummying on his right. Big Anthony (Tohill) was standing directly in front of the goals and I remember soon after the ball left Johnny's foot, Anthony raised his two fists to the air. He was in no doubt and I was watching him rather than watching the ball go over.'

Derry held on and McGurk had the ball in his hands, ready to take a sideline kick, when the final whistle went. It was as good a game as anyone could wish for with as good a winning point as Croke Park had ever seen.

'A Derry team had never gone down to Croke Park and come back like that against one of the so-called big teams. We got a lot of confidence from that, but we knew that it wasn't the final yet. Things could still go wrong.'

Cork would provide the opposition in the final, but that was still a month away – plenty of time for a county to lose the run of itself. A Maghera man, Gormley was right in the middle of the mayhem.

'It was bedlam, but it was bedlam right through the year. I remember being interviewed by the BBC before the Ulster final and the whole of Maghera was decked out in red and white. The players had an obsession about winning, but so did the whole county.

'A momentum had been building over two years since we won the league in 1992. Donegal beat us that year, but beating Down in the first round in '93 lit the fuse again. It went from mad to worse and after we beat Dublin it went loo-lah. I was glad to get to training to get away from it sometimes because you were having the same conversation twenty times a day.'

As the final approached, Gormley had his own problems. The week before

Brian McGilligan's midfield partnership with Anthony Tohill was the foundation of Derry's 1993 All-Ireland success. Here McGilligan sets up another Derry attack as Dublin's Jack Sheedy can only look on during the All-Ireland semi-final

the game he picked up a flu bug and got progressively weaker as Sunday neared. As the team's principal free-taker and top scorer, he had to be fit. He wasn't even close, but wasn't going to miss his All-Ireland chance.

'I didn't tell anybody, but I was definitely touch and go. I remember leaving the house on Saturday morning and I wasn't in great shape at all. I thought it might be nerves, but I was never the type to get nervous too early before a game. Maybe in the changing rooms or something, but never the day before. On that Saturday I felt as weak as water and I remember going down to get the bus and, from our house to the chapel where the bus was, would be about five hundred or six hundred metres. It must have taken three quarters of an hour to get through it, with people stopping you and wishing you luck. That totally drained me.

'I took on a lot of fluids, but I couldn't eat a bite of the lunch we had; but

Dublin's Paul Bealin and Derry's Anthony Tohill contest possession in the All-Ireland semi-final

Seamus Downey and Mark O'Connor fight for possession as Damian Barton looks on during the 1993 final

I was never going to miss the match. It was something I had dreamed of and I wasn't going to miss it.'

The Derry team stayed out at Dublin Airport before the game and, as the bus made its way towards Croke Park, the thousands of Derry supporters gave their ailing corner-forward the lift he needed.

'It helped when we were coming into Croke Park on the Sunday and the bus hit the crowds and the cheering. That revitalised me. Coming in you could recognise people in the crowds and that gave you another lift. It's one of the great things about the GAA, especially in a small GAA community like Derry.'

Croke Park was painted red and white for the day, but it was clear that Derry colours outnumbered those from Cork. As the teams paraded round the stadium, Gormley picked out some familiar faces in the crowd as he took up the rear in the Derry line.

'I remember noticing a few boys from home. I went through stages in my career of ignoring the crowd and looking round, but at that stage I just thought, "Enjoy it, you might not be back."'

Derry started atrociously. First Tony Davis pointed five minutes in, then Joe Kavanagh went straight through the heart of the Derry defence to score a goal. Colin Corkery added a free a minute later, all against the wind. Johnny McGurk finally got Derry off the mark with a point in the seventh minute.

'It's not the way you want to start an All-Ireland final. The one thing in our favour was that we had been there before at half-time against Dublin, but we needed that first score and Johnny McGurk came up and got what I think was the most important score of the day. That really settled us.

Dermot McNicholl thumps the ball towards goal amid the raindrops in the 1993 final

'We were always confident, but it was like any game – you can't think about it too much, you just get on with it. We had overcome so much in the years before that we weren't going to throw it in after a bad start.'

Points followed from Brian McGilligan, Gormley and Anthony Tohill, Tohill's from a 'forty-five' after John Kerins saved well from Damien Cassidy. A minute later Cassidy hit a speculative lob from the Hogan Stand side of the field towards the Cork square. Mark O'Connor and Kerins both froze as Seamus Downey barrelled in between them to fist to the net and reward Derry with the lead. Tohill pointed again in the eighteenth minute, completing an unanswered 1-5 scoring run. Shay Fahy got one back for Cork and Damien McCusker needed to be alert to stop a point-blank shot from Michael McCarthy a minute later. Corkery and Gormley exchanged frees before Joe Brolly got on the scoresheet with Derry's seventh point in the twenty-fourth minute. Kavanagh and Corkery pulled two more back for Cork, but Derry were still leading, even if Gormley wasn't having the best of days.

'Personally I had a desperate start and couldn't do anything right. I think I was looking over my shoulder to see if somebody else would be coming on.'

Ironically, if he had been looking over his shoulder four minutes from half-time, he would have seen Niall Cahalane's left hook coming. Television replays clearly showed the Cork corner-back thumping Gormley, who was off the ball, on the jaw from behind.

'It annoyed me that, in a few interviews afterwards he said, "If you kick a dog often enough it will bite you back", or something like that, but I hadn't said a word to him, good or bad. You can accept it if you get hit man to man, but not like that. It wasn't the hardest slap I've been hit, but I simply didn't see it coming. Even if you saw it at the last minute you could brace yourself a bit, but the first I knew of it I was in a heap on the ground.'

After consulting his umpires, referee Tommy Howard decided a booking was fitting punishment and Cahalane somehow stayed on the field. Gormley managed to pick himself up and score Derry's last two points of the half, the first a superb effort from under the Hogan Stand, the second when he punched Gary Coleman's rebound over the bar to see his team off the field with a 1-9 to 1-6 interval advantage.

Cork did go in at the break with fourteen men, but it was Tony Davis, rather than Cahalane, who saw red for a rash, but not particularly bad challenge on Dermot Heaney. Davis seemed to be paying for Cahalane's sin.

'After Tommy Howard booked Cahalane I lost the head and I was lucky not to get into trouble because I grabbed his jersey. I was pointing to my jaw and there must have been a mark on it because his (the referee's) expression changed, and I think he realised he had goofed by not sending Cahalane off. Tony Davis maybe paid the price for it. It was a rash tackle, but I don't think it was a sending-off. I think it was balancing the books a bit.'

Unlike the semi-final against Dublin, there was no fire and brimstone at half-time in the Derry changing room, but that didn't mean they thought the job was done.

'At half-time we were still up against it because there was a bit of a breeze, but we knew we were good enough. We talked about that and what we had gone through over the years, and that we couldn't let it go. At that point it was a case of concentrating and realising that it was our best chance to win an All-Ireland.'

Two Corkery frees sandwiched a Dermott McNicholl point after the break and Derry's lead was cut to two. It was wiped out altogether when Don Davis split the Derry defence with a brilliant crossfield pass to John O'Driscoll, who fired low past McCusker. Derry were behind, but they didn't panic, while Cork didn't score again.

'After they got the goal we had a fair bit of possession, but there were no scores for maybe five or ten minutes. We had two or three attacks, but didn't get anything from them. Eventually Dermot Heaney made a great run, drew Cahalane and made an easy score for me. We got the equaliser, then pushed on and went two or three up. That obsession that I talked about was there and we just weren't going to lose it.'

Cork kept their opponents at bay for the next ten minutes with a combination of poor Derry finishing, the woodwork, and solid play from John Kerins. Gormley finally drew Derry level after fifty-five minutes and Tohill put over a free to take back the lead two minutes later.

Cork were making little headway, and McGurk and Gormley pushed Derry's lead out to three points with five minutes left. They didn't need any more scores and packed their defence to prevent the goal Cork needed to get back into the game. Gormley looked on in horror as one Cork attack swept down the field.

'Tommy Howard thought I spent too long taking a free kick and they got the ball, went down the field and hit the ball less than a foot wide. We had a fair few men on the line, but when that shot went in I could see the rest of my life with me being the man who lost Derry the All-Ireland. I was never as glad to see a ball go wide in my life.'

Cork continued to push. There was still time for one last assault, as well as one last crafty move from Derry manager Eamonn Coleman.

'Their last attack was from a sideline ball twenty-five or thirty yards from our goals. We packed the square, and I was in front of whoever was trying to hit the kick and wouldn't let him. Then, from behind, Coleman nicked the ball from under his arm. We weren't going to let them hit a quick kick.'

When the kick finally went in, Derry's defence, now numbering fifteen, cleared the danger and the final whistle crowned them All-Ireland champions. Gormley's thoughts turned to the people he knew best.

'I was next to Fergal McCusker, a club-mate, and we'd been playing football all our lives together. We jumped on each other and Don Davis was in between us and, God love him, we jumped on him as well. We didn't mean any insult to him, but it was just madness.

'One of my inspirations growing up was my uncle, Colm Mullan, who was paralysed in a car crash. I ran straight over to him below Hill 16 where he was. The crowd was running off the Hill and I was going in the opposite direction, but by that stage there were so many Derry shirts, and everybody was soaking, that nobody recognised you. When I tried to get back through the crowd to the presentation area people were telling you to bugger off, that they were there first.'

He finally made it back to the Hogan Stand to see Henry Downey lifting Sam and joined the Derry panel in celebrating becoming Joe Brolly's immortals.

Derry's obsessive fifteen in 1993 were:

DERRY 1993
Damien McCusker
Kieran McKeever — Tony Scullion — Fergal McCusker
Johnny McGurk — Henry Downey — Gary Coleman
Anthony Tohill — Brian McGilligan
Dermot Heaney — Damian Barton — Damien Cassidy
Joe Brolly — Seamus Downey — Enda Gormley
Substitutes
Dermot McNicholl for Damien Cassidy; Eamonn Burns for Seamus Downey

'We had spent so much time together,' says Gormley, 'and been through so much together we were a big family and just wanted to be together. Nothing was sinking in, it was just like you were floating.'

The flu wasn't bothering him anymore, either.

'Everything I had taken and all the euphoria carried me through to the Friday after the final and I just crashed, I couldn't move. The first weekend off in twenty weeks and I was home in bed.'

The adrenaline was still flowing the morning after the final and Gormley enjoyed waking up as an All-Ireland champion.

'That was the best feeling of the lot. I couldn't get up quick enough to see what was going on in the hotel and talk to people. That feeling was there for weeks. You couldn't be insulted, nothing else mattered.'

The homecoming took in the usual stops on the way north: Drogheda, Dundalk and Newry, but followed a new route through Armagh, Moy, Dungannon and Cookstown. It was nice to be appreciated in Armagh and Tyrone, but Gormley and his team-mates couldn't wait to be back home in Derry.

'The first bit of peace I managed to get was at the Carrickdale Hotel when myself and Henry Downey were taken away to do a live interview for the TV. The hotel had a bit of space cordoned off and we were able to sit down for a bit and just take it all in.

'It was good to see the impression we had made outside the county but, being selfish, you just wanted to get back to your own. All day we just wanted to get home. It was nice, but we were really just stuck in the back of a bus, couldn't even get a drink, and it was an oul wet winter's night. The windows were steamed up and we couldn't even see out them.'

The final destination that night was Gormley's home town of Maghera and the bus finally arrived at almost 3am. The streets had been packed with people all afternoon and it seemed that no one had gone home. Gormley's father Joe was in the middle of it all.

'My father had a bar in Maghera and he always talks about a fella from Kerry who had come up for the celebrations. He asked for a pint, but the bar was totally packed and my father told him he would have to get a glass himself, then my father could wash it and give him a pint.

'The man smiled and said, "I have this problem every year", and turned and walked out the bar. Next thing he comes back with a big cardboard box and sets it on the bar. It was full of pint glasses. Every year this man went to whatever county won the All-Ireland with the pint glasses he knew would be needed. It would take a Kerryman to think of that and he was well looked after that night.'

That it was a homecoming in every sense for Enda Gormley made the moment more special than he could have dreamed. Derry's All-Ireland odyssey had consumed the lives of everyone connected to the team.

'It's not just a big thing in a football sense because it takes over your whole life and your family. They go through so much as well, and they experience

*Henry Downey lifts
the Sam Maguire*

the highs and lows and are kicking every ball with you. My father just couldn't get enough of it. My mother refused to go to a match all year, but said she would go to the final, probably never believing that we would get there. At the same time, she knew everything that was happening, every player that was injured, who was playing well. It was the only thing talked about in the house for weeks.

'To carry the Sam Maguire on an open-top bus past thousands of people, past your own house, with your family standing outside is something that, it if you dreamed it when you were a child, you'd say it was far-fetched.

'We used to laugh because there was a fella who was a great club supporter of ours, John McMath. He used to talk about the open-top bus going through Maghera, carrying a county championship or an All-Ireland when I was a cub of ten or twelve years of age. To me then it was just pie in the sky stuff, but there it was. His words had come true.'

Man of the Match:
Anthony Tohill
Probably the first people to get a glimpse of how good Anthony Tohill would become were those present at the 1989 MacRory Cup final between St Patrick's, Maghera and St Colman's, Newry. The young man propelled the Maghera team to a 4-10 to 4-9 victory, the first of many wins he would inspire for Derry sides over the next fourteen years. Maghera went on to win the Hogan Cup in 1989, and later that year Tohill picked up an All-Ireland minor medal.

The lure of Australian Rules football took him Down Under the following year and, when he returned to Ireland in 1991, Eamonn Coleman drafted him into the Derry senior set-up. His late 1-1 gave Derry an unlikely 1992 National League final win over Tyrone, but disappointment followed when the Oak Leafers lost the 1992 Ulster final to Donegal. Tohill missed the second half of that match after picking up a self-inflicted injury, breaking a bone in his foot in a clumsy tackle on Tony Boyle.

1993 was earmarked as Derry's year, and it started well for Tohill when he helped Queen's University win the Sigerson Cup. As the summer went on he put in one outstanding performance after another to help Derry first to the Ulster title, then into the All-Ireland final, and finally to ultimate glory against Cork.

Tohill formed a powerful midfield partnership with Brian McGilligan, providing his team with an aerial presence, a scoring threat, a very reliable long-range free taker, and a real leader on the field. That year he was honoured with his second successive All-Star award; he was to gain two more before he was finished, as well as another Ulster title in 1998. Three more National League ribbons and four Railway Cup medals were added to his tally, all of this being achieved at a time when Tohill was recognised as Ulster's best footballer, and Ulster football was the best in the country.

Anthony Tohill takes on Down's Conor Deegan, and wins the ball handsomely

9

'It's Nice to be the Best'

ARMAGH 2002

'In the interests of safety, patrons will not be allowed to enter the playing area after the game.'

Even the most optimistic Armagh supporter would have paid little attention to the now customary announcement ringing from the Croke Park public address system at half-time in the 2002 All-Ireland final. Their team was four points down against Kerry – in truth lucky to be so close – and looked to have lost their chance. Against all the odds, however, the final whistle heralded an orange invasion of the pitch.

By the time captain Kieran McGeeney scaled the Hogan Stand steps to accept the Sam Maguire there was some concern at the crush developing below him. McGeeney immediately took charge.

'Listen, listen!' he bellowed into the microphone. 'Listen. Push back, you're hurting the ones at the front, so push back. Push back. C'mon everybody move back. Please, just move back. Listen, I'm not going to keep youse.'

The thousands on the field didn't need to be asked twice. They dutifully shuffled back as one, easing the pressure, and allowing McGeeney to become the first Armagh man to address GAA headquarters on receiving the Sam Maguire. If it seemed an unlikely prospect at half-time, twelve months before it had appeared almost unbelievable.

Brian Canavan and Brian McAlinden stepped down as joint Armagh managers soon after their championship exit to Galway in 2001. Under the 'Two Brians' Armagh won Ulster titles in 1999 and 2000, and had developed into one of the top teams in the country. When it came to Croke Park, however, they just couldn't win.

In the 1999 All-Ireland semi-final two first half goals gave them hope against Meath, but they couldn't hang on. At the same stage in 2000 Kerry needed extra time in a replay before finally seeing off the Ulster challenge. Galway was the opposition the next year at Croke Park in the new All-Ireland qualifiers, but the result was the same. Each year, Armagh's conquerors went on to win the All-Ireland.

The Galway loss was particularly hard to take. After the westerners had built up a seven-point lead with less than twenty minutes remaining, Armagh hauled themselves back into the game and were level with time running out. Justin McNulty had possession for Armagh and prepared to launch the ball into his forwards. Galway's Michael Donnellan blocked his kick, gathered the ball, then passed to Paul Clancy who slotted over the winner. Another year and another Croke Park heartbreak for Armagh. McNulty cut a distraught figure after the match. He sank to the turf and buried his head in his hands, knowing many would blame him for his side's defeat. A few newspapers did exactly that the next day, but just over a year later he grabbed his chance of redemption when he snuffed out three Kerry attacks in the last ten minutes of the game to preserve Armagh's lead, and their All-Ireland.

Few would have predicted McNulty's, and Armagh's, change in fortune, even when Joe Kernan took over as manager in November 2001. On the field Kernan had won All-Star awards in 1977 and 1982, while he had made his name as a manager by leading Crossmaglen Rangers to All-Ireland Club titles in 1997, 1999 and 2000.

All-Ireland champions-to-be don't usually spend the spring gracing venues like Ruislip and Aughrim, but Armagh's relegation in 2000 meant that Kernan had to guide his new charges through Division 2A of the National League. At least they had Kerry for company and, en route to reclaiming their top-flight place, their only defeat came against Páidí Ó Sé's side in Tralee. They missed out on a chance for quick revenge against Kerry when Laois surprisingly booked a Division Two final place against the Kingdom by beating Armagh in the semi-final. Another shot at Kerry would have to wait.

While Armagh were plodding through Division Two, neighbours Tyrone were tearing through Division One, eventually securing the county's first senior national title by beating Cavan in the all-Ulster decider in Clones. Tyrone's superb play in lifting the league crown had made them one of the counties fancied for All-Ireland honours and favourites for the Ulster title. In a time when managers and players do their best to hype up the opposition and play down their own chances, Armagh couldn't have been happier with the wave of adulation and expectation that engulfed Tyrone. The counties met at Clones on 19 May.

Brendan Tierney was in goal for Armagh that day, despite having retired after the 2001 championship when he lost his place to Paul Hearty. The Mullaghbawn man's last championship game had been against Tyrone at the same venue twelve months before, when his first act was to retrieve the ball Owen Mulligan shot to his net after less than ten seconds. Tierney lost his place to Paul Hearty for Armagh's next three championship games and, when Galway ended their summer, he decided to hang up his gloves. When Joe

Kernan took up the Armagh reins he wanted Tierney on board, but the primary school teacher wasn't for turning.

'I was gone,' remembers Tierney. 'Joe rang me and said they were drawing up a panel for the year, and said they wanted me to be involved. I told him no, I had made up my mind, I was quitting. He asked if there was anything he could say or do. I said, "Tell me I'll play." He told me he couldn't do that. He asked if he could meet me and I told him it wouldn't make much difference, but he insisted and came to see me the next day. He told me that we would meet in a year's time and I wouldn't be able to talk to him because Armagh will have won the All-Ireland, and I won't have been a part of it.

'I didn't give him an answer and he said he would give me a couple of days to think about it. He phoned one Saturday morning and I told him, "I don't know, I have to discuss it with the family", and he said, "OK, leave it." He phoned thirty seconds later and just said, "What the fuck's going on? Are you a man or not? You're in or you're out."

'I was taken aback by that and he told me to come for a week and go if I didn't like it, but we both knew that if I came back for a week that was me back.'

Before Armagh got to Clones, they went to La Manga in Spain for a training camp – a move that caused a stir in the media, among supporters, and not least the panel itself. While Tierney liked the idea of a week in the sun, he wasn't so sure how the news would be received outside the camp.

'I thought it was a major gamble. It wouldn't have been as much of a gamble if we had won an All-Ireland two or three years previously and needed to freshen things up, but for a team that had never won an All-Ireland it was a major gamble.

'Obviously we were all up for it when we were told. I had visions of sipping cocktails on a sandy beach with dusky maidens walking by and all that, but the reality was something totally different. I remember the Tyrone ones the first day asking, "Where's the tan?" and all that. If we had been beaten that day La Manga would have been the running joke of all jokes. It bonded us as a team and Joe got an edge out of that. He got to know players that he maybe wouldn't have gotten to know through just training at home. It was a masterstroke in hindsight.'

While not quite La Manga, it was a beautiful day in Clones when Armagh and Tyrone served up a brilliantly entertaining game of football. For the first thirty-five minutes the teams went toe-to-toe, virtually point-for-point, and went in level at 0-6 each at the break.

The sides had 0-10 each in the second half when Steven McDonnell collected a long punt forward from John Toal before finding the net. Substitute Ronan Clarke tacked on another point to give Armagh a 1-11 to 0-10 lead.

Tyrone poured forward, but were still three points behind with time running out when Sean Cavanagh collected a high ball from Colin Holmes and shot to the net. That wasn't the end of the drama, however. Peter

After Derry's Ulster championship preliminary round hiding from Tyrone, nobody would have predicted they would get further than the All-Ireland title-holders. Here, Derry's Jonny McBride and Paddy Bradley combine to keep the ball away from Tyrone's Enda McGinley and Gavin Devlin

Fermanagh were not expected to get anywhere near Tyrone in their Ulster championship clash, but their battling performance was a sign of things to come. Brian McGuigan is seen here under pressure from Eamon Maguire

Tyrone's Ryan McMenamin fends off a spectacular attack from Fermanagh's Raymond Johnston

Tyrone were the victors in their Ulster championship encounter with Fermanagh, but the Ernemen were justifiably proud of their performance in a match that was far from one-sided

Armagh were keen to avenge their loss to Monaghan a year earlier, and did so in emphatic style in Clones. James Coyle tries to get to grips with Ronan Clarke

Antrim's Sean Kelly and Anto Finnegan cannot stop Donegal's Adrian Sweeney setting up another attack during the sides' Ulster championship meeting in Ballybofey

Cavan and Down produced two thrilling games at the start of the summer, with the Breffni men coming out on top after a replay. Cavan's Michael Lyng flies past Down's Dan Gordon and Eoin McCartan during the first game in Casement Park

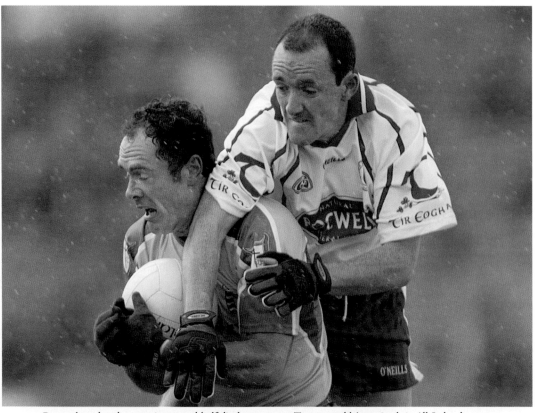

Donegal produced a stunning second half display to ensure Tyrone wouldn't retain their All-Ireland crown.
Damian Diver shields the ball from Brian Dooher during their Ulster semi-final

Damian Diver blocks a shot from Armagh's Diarmaid Marsden during the Croke Park Ulster final

Fermanagh captain Shane McDermott tries to escape the clutches of Armagh duo Aidan O'Rourke and Tony McEntee

Mayo's Ronan McGarrity pushes Tyrone's Sean Cavanagh away from the ball during the sides' All-Ireland quarter-final. Mayo proved a bridge too far for Mickey Harte's team, who surrendered their All-Ireland crown

Along with Enda Muldoon, Paddy Bradley was Derry's chief destroyer in their All-Ireland quarter-final win over Westmeath. Damien Healy can't catch him this time

Derry's James Donaghy leaves his feet and takes possession against Westmeath

*Fermanagh's Stephen Maguire
fends off a challenge from
Mayo's James Nallan during
the All-Ireland semi-final*

*Fermanagh's Mark Little
on his way past Mayo's
Fergal Kelly*

Canavan – as good a forward as there has ever been – took possession with a point seemingly at his mercy. Instead of kicking his score the Tyrone captain elected to pass to Richard Thornton on his inside. That split second was all Tierney needed to close the space and force Thornton to shoot high and wide. Tierney was glad he got the chance to close that space.

'I've slagged Peter about it, asked him what the hell was going on, told him, "You knew I would save it." Nine times out of ten he would have put it over, but he saw a man in a better position and he gave it to him, but Thornton turned his back on him at the last minute. If that had went over the whole story might have been different, but that's the way football goes. To win an All-Ireland you need a fair share of luck and we got it in that game and a few others.'

The replay a week later was probably even better than the first game. Donegal All-Ireland winner Martin McHugh described it as the best he had ever seen, bar the astonishing Down v Derry encounter in 1994. Both sides made changes. For Armagh, Francie Bellew was preferred to Paul McCormack at the back, while Ronan Clarke came in for Tony McEntee to make his first championship start. Tyrone made just one change, but the enforced absence of their captain and talisman Canavan, who had been injured early on in the first game, was a huge blow to their chances.

Like the previous encounter, momentum swung constantly between the sides. Armagh got the first three points, Tyrone kicked the next six, then Armagh scored 1-5 without reply to leave the pitch on 1-8 to 0-6 at half-time. Their goal had come courtesy of John McEntee just before the break.

Tyrone regrouped again in the second half and eventually hauled themselves level through Brian McGuigan, but Armagh's reply was immediate and decisive. Oisin McConville found substitute Barry Duffy unmarked and fired past Peter Ward to put a goal between the sides. Tyrone were spent and Armagh finished 2-13 to 0-16 in front.

After the hype and excitement of the Tyrone games, Armagh's semi-final against Fermanagh was something of a letdown. Fermanagh had earned a shot at Armagh with a 4-13 to 2-11 win over Monaghan, in which Rory Gallagher collected a record-breaking personal haul of 3-9.

While Armagh were well aware of Fermanagh's capabilities – there was only a point between the sides at the end of the 2000 Ulster semi-final – Tierney acknowledges that it was difficult to keep the motivation levels up.

Fermanagh's Paddy McGuinness feels the pressure from Diarmaid Marsden during the Ulster semi-final in 2002

'When you're training the week before a Tyrone match you are giving it everything, busting a gut, thinking about it every night. The week before playing Fermanagh your mind is off the ball a wee bit. You don't have good training sessions. While the likes of Kieran McGeeney will train at one

hundred per cent all the time, other players might not be quite so focused than if they were playing Tyrone, which makes it uncomfortable.

'When you get to the game there isn't the same atmosphere or crowd and, while you don't underestimate them, playing Fermanagh is not the same as playing Tyrone or Down.'

In the end Armagh accounted for Fermanagh comfortably, running out 0-16 to 1-5 winners. Gallagher was held scoreless from play, while his county didn't manage a second half point until he converted a seventieth minute penalty. The main damage was done after the break when Armagh, leading just 0-5 to 0-4 at the interval, outscored Fermanagh 0-11 to 1-1.

Although Armagh eventually won the Ulster final against Donegal by four points, they probably should have lost, not for the first – or last – time that summer. Donegal's normally reliable forwards kicked wide after wide in the first half, but they still managed to pull level, 0-4 to 1-1, after twelve minutes. They should have been ahead, as Armagh's goal, after just two minutes, came when Donegal goalkeeper Tony Blake misjudged a bouncing ball in his square that was eventually palmed to the net by John McEntee.

Armagh went in a goal up at half-time, 1-6 to 0-6, and got the first point of the second half from Steven McDonnell, but Donegal continued to miss scoreable chances. Ronan Clarke extended the Armagh lead to five points with fourteen minutes left, then Jim McGuinness threw Donegal a lifeline with a fine goal after a seven-pass move.

That was as close as Donegal would get. Armagh held on, with a couple more points to spare, to claim the county's third Ulster title in four years. While Kernan's first trophy as a county manager was more than welcome, it wasn't difficult to tell that he and his squad had bigger prizes on their minds.

Winning their provincial championship meant Armagh would face a qualifier in the All-Ireland quarter-finals. The possibilities were Kerry, Mayo and Sligo, who had surprisingly beaten Tyrone in the previous round. Tierney's feeling when he discovered Armagh had been paired with the Connacht side mirrored those of their supporters.

'I can remember getting the word that it was Sligo, sitting in the house. And while I didn't get on the phone and say, "Woo-hoo, it's Sligo!" that's the way I felt. There were massive teams left and we needed a good draw because we needed to get back into an All-Ireland semi-final, and Kerry probably wouldn't have done us any good at that stage.'

The game was in Croke Park and gave Armagh the chance to shake the 'hoodoo' that supposedly struck them when they played at GAA headquarters. They had managed just a draw in their last six championship visits to Croke Park. Their last win had been in the 1977 semi-final replay against Roscommon. As it turned out, Sligo gave Armagh as many problems as Kerry would in the All-Ireland final, and the 'hoodoo' lived to haunt another day. Steven McDonnell's goal after twenty-one minutes was the highlight of a steady first half display. Then, just after the break, Diarmaid Marsden added another goal, John McEntee scored and Armagh were seven

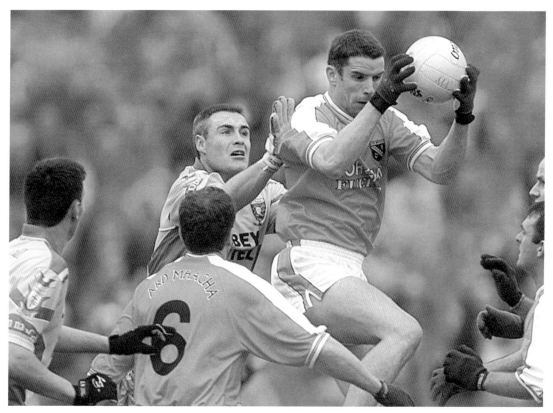

Donegal's John Gildea can't stop Paul McGrane taking possession in the Ulster final

points up and cruising. Suddenly, the wheels came off. Armagh found it almost impossible to create chances and scoring proved beyond them for the last twenty-two minutes of play.

Sligo wing-back David Durkin was sent off in the fifty-eighth minute but, instead of capitalising, Armagh became disjointed, unorganised, and started to panic. 'It was just a total collapse,' recalls Tierney.

'It was one of the few games that I can remember feeling comfortable during until ten or fifteen minutes before the finish when I just thought, "What in the name of sweet God is going on here?" Everything had been going to plan; then, all of a sudden, panic ensued.'

Sligo had dragged Armagh's lead back to just a point when full-back Justin McNulty's hand-pass was intercepted by Dara McGarty, who bore down on goal with just Tierney to beat. After Peter Canavan in Clones, the Armagh goalkeeper felt a dose of *déjà vu* coming on.

'I remember thinking, "He's going for goal", and I could never understand why he fisted the ball because the goal was on and he had the chance to win the game. But after looking at it again he took his eye off the ball when he bounced it and it bounced a little high. I think he took the right option in the end.'

McGarty fisted the ball over the bar to equalise the scores at 0-15 to 2-9, but there was still time for Eamon O'Hara, who would win an All-Star award at the end of the season, to get the ball in midfield.

Ronan Clarke sneaks past Sligo's Neil Carew in the All-Ireland quarter-final

'Eamon O'Hara had a shot as well and he kicked it about thirty yards wide, but when he had the ball in his hands I remember thinking, "That's that. Why the fuck did I come back?" You could see the headlines the next day: "Hoodoo strikes again."'

With Croke Park unavailable due to the All-Ireland hurling semi-finals, the replay was fixed for Navan, where there was no 'hoodoo' and, on the day, not too many Armagh supporters. A fraction of the travelling followers who had gone to Croke Park made the journey to the less glamorous surroundings of Pairc Tailteann in the Meath town. The players noticed the difference, but got on with the job.

'A lot was made about the venue and our supporters didn't turn up, and we always said before the semi-final with Dublin that we were going to do it for the supporters that went to Navan. It didn't matter to us. I've played in a lot worse places than Navan and we were trying to get to an All-Ireland semi-final. It didn't matter where the game was being played.'

Like the first game, Armagh did the damage just after half-time, swelling a two-point interval lead to seven points two minutes into the second half. Ronan Clarke scored a point and a goal in quick succession and, unlike the first game, Armagh delivered the odd counter-punch to Sligo's attacks. The Connacht men did eat into the lead, but Armagh always looked like they were capable of staying out of the trouble that had nearly ended their championship in the drawn game, and finished 1-16 to 0-17 to the good.

Armagh were back in an All-Ireland semi-final and were paired with Dublin for the counties' first championship meeting since the Dubs easily beat them in the 1977 final.

Like Donegal, Derry and Down at the start of the 1990s, Armagh were confronted with a Dublin team hyped way above their station by the media in the capital. They had won their first Leinster championship since 1995 – the year they beat Tyrone in the All-Ireland final – and hammered Donegal in the All-Ireland quarter-final replay, albeit after a lucky escape on the first day.

The fact that Kerry had booked their place in the final a week earlier meant that Armagh weren't just facing a Dublin bandwagon, but a 'Dublin–Kerry final' bandwagon, which was gathering ridiculous momentum in the media outside Ulster. While Tierney wouldn't normally be one to let what the media thinks get to him, he admits that one piece in particular, by former Meath star Colm O'Rourke, did get under his skin.

'I remember reading Colm O'Rourke in the *Sunday Independent* on the morning of the game saying even the taxi drivers and bus drivers and people who don't follow GAA know it's going to be a Dublin v Kerry final. I just thought: "You arrogant bastard."'

Comments like that gave Armagh the extra incentive they hardly needed and, when they took to Croke Park on Sunday, 1 September, they were greeted by the awesome sight of nearly 80,000 people, almost all of whom seemed to be waving sky blue or orange flags.

'The atmosphere at the semi was better than at the final. I think any Armagh player would tell you that. What you had at that game was a ground packed with die-hard supporters. As a player I will remember the way the supporters got behind us. You rarely hear a crowd, but I heard a crowd that day. The noise lifted and lifted. You knew you were part of something special.'

Kernan had something special planned for half-time. When the players filed into the dressing room, their manager showed them the jersey he had worn in the 1977 All-Ireland final against Dublin. He told them he wanted them to wear the orange jersey in an All-Ireland final.

'Joe has great respect for the county jersey. He doesn't like us swapping it after games and he sees it as a very important thing to be given before every match. Joe is a great speaker at half-time and I wouldn't be the best listener, but I listen to Joe. Paul Grimley (the assistant manager) is good too. He would be more of a fire-and-brimstone type, while Joe would calm it down a bit more. They are a very good double act.'

Dublin sprinted off the blocks and were three points up before Paddy McKeever got Armagh on the board in the tenth minute. The Ulster

champions followed with two more and scores were exchanged until Oisin McConville bagged an equaliser to make it 0-6 apiece just before half-time.

Steven McDonnell and Senan Connell traded points at the start of the half; then both sides swapped goals in the space of a minute. First, McKeever bundled into the net, but Dublin replied forty-nine seconds later when Ciaran Whelan smashed in from twenty metres. As soon as Whelan struck Tierney knew where it was going, but he was equally sure it didn't mean the end of Armagh's chances.

'I knew the moment he hit it that it was in. As a keeper you just know when you're beaten. I was maybe waiting for the distant sound of the crossbar to take it back out, but I knew it was past me. But I still thought it was our day. We were playing well and hitting points.'

Dublin pushed two points clear on three occasions in the twenty minutes after the goal, but Armagh replied within ninety seconds each time. They were a point behind with five minutes left when Darren Homan wasted a chance to extend Dublin's lead to two again. His weak shot fell into the hands of Tierney, who started a five-pass move that ended with John McEntee bringing both sides level at 1-13 each. Then, McConville gave Armagh the advantage when he fisted over. Dublin threw everything at Armagh to keep their championship going. With time virtually up, Ray Cosgrove won a free from Enda McNulty. Memories of 2000, when Maurice Fitzgerald saved Kerry with a late free in the All-Ireland semi-final, entered Tierney's mind.

'That's when the self doubt creeps in again. I didn't think he would miss it. He had been having such a good year; he was in front of the Hill and everything else. I remember thinking it was going over and that a replay isn't the worst thing in the world, but I was also worrying about the kick-out and wondering where I was going to put it.'

Just as Tierney had been sure of the destination of Ciaran Whelan's kick when it left his boot, he knew where Cosgrove's was, or rather wasn't, going.

'When he kicked it I knew it wasn't going over. You can tell after seeing so many points going over you. That was hit about six feet to the right of the posts and would have needed a massive curl to come back. I was shouting, "Post! Post! Post!" I didn't know it was going to hit it, but I shout "Post" if it's going five or six yards wide. When it came down there were five or six Armagh men there. There was no way a Dub was going to get that ball.'

Justin McNulty batted the rebound away and Kieran Hughes ended up with the ball when Michael Collins blew the whistle to put Armagh into their third All-Ireland final. The players embraced and enjoyed the moment, something the post-final pitch invasion prevented, and Tierney acknowledges that the semi-final provided a different type of celebration: one for the players to enjoy themselves. The next celebration would be for Armagh people everywhere.

The day after the semi-final Tierney returned to work for the new year at St Mary's Primary School in Mullaghbawn. He got quite a welcome.

'Mr Tierney suddenly became very popular. The kids were unbelievable. I loved talking about it and the kids loved asking questions. I knew it was the last throw of the dice so I didn't mind talking to anyone who asked.'

It wasn't just Mr Tierney's Primary 7s asking questions. The interest in the Armagh camp and the unlikely final pairing was huge. Some players were more comfortable staying out of the spotlight in the run-up to the final, while others, like Tierney, lapped it up. Kernan made sure his team was accessible to fans and the media, but not to the detriment of the preparations. Kerry's approach was markedly different, with Páidí Ó Sé all but hiding his players from journalists. Even if Armagh's accessibility won them friends among the media, sentimentality didn't colour the predictions, with most plumping for Kerry. It didn't particularly bother Tierney, who could see their point.

'I always read the press. It wouldn't matter what it was, I would read it. There might be something you remember like the O'Rourke stuff, but with most of it, you just read it and say, "Fair enough". To be honest, if I was a reporter and not an Armagh man, I probably would have tipped Kerry.'

The weekend before the final Kernan took the panel to the Citywest Hotel on the outskirts of Dublin and went through the routine they would experience a week later. The players stayed in the same rooms, ate the same food at the same time, trained and met at the same time as they would before the final. Nothing would be new, at least not until they got into Dublin on Sunday, 22 September.

As the team bus approached Croke Park on final day Tierney was beginning to feel butterflies, but he needn't have worried. He had Tony McEntee sitting beside him.

'Tony McEntee denies this ever happened, but it did. We were coming round the corner at Quinn's bar and saw a sea of orange and white, and I turned to Tony, who's the most laid back person you've ever met. I said, "Holy fuck, Tony. Have you ever seen anything like it?" "I know, Benny," he replied. "Did you ever see so much talent in your life?"

'There I was, I was shitting myself at the enormity of it all and the occasion, and there was Tony McEntee checking out the blonde outside the pub, or whatever. But that was the end of the nerves.

'It is something I've dreamed of. I remember 1977. I went to the semi-final with my dad and remember crying because I couldn't get tickets to the final. I remember at half-time going out to the garden and being Brian McAlinden, Paddy Mo (Paddy Moriarty) and boys like that. It was a dream come true. But there was also that feeling that it wasn't worth a fuck if we didn't win it.'

Derry's minors got the day off to a good start for Ulster when they comfortably, and very impressively, beat Meath in their final. The Armagh players grabbed a few minutes of the game before going to prepare for their own All-Ireland. They emerged from the Hogan Stand to a burst of colour and noise – mainly orange, Armagh noise. Kieran McGeeney led his team to the Canal End goal to meet President Mary McAleese and around Croke Park in the parade. Tierney loved every minute of the pre-match pomp and circumstance.

'I tend to soak it all up and enjoy it. I don't go out with a steely glare, but I am focused. It was a break to meet Mary McAleese and these are things you see people doing year in, year out and say, "I wish I was doing that."

'I can remember one point when the legs were a wee bit wobbly. Paul McGrane always stands beside me in the photograph and he won't join the photograph until I get there. I was particularly slow getting to the photograph and I remember saying to him, "I don't think I'm fit for this", and he laughed. I can't remember Paul McGrane laughing before a game in my life and I just thought, "Things are going to be alright."'

Things started very well for Armagh, and they were 0-3 to 0-1 up after four minutes thanks to two points from Steven McDonnell and one from Ronan Clarke. The latter, at nineteen years of age, would go on to thoroughly outplay Seamus Moynihan, widely regarded as the best player in the country. Kerry replied with four unanswered points and things were looking a little ominous for the Armagh full-back line, picked out as a weakness by many before the game. Colm Cooper and Mike Frank Russell both scored points while Justin McNulty found himself chasing Dara Ó Cinnéide all over the field.

Armagh regained the lead through points from Clarke and John McEntee, but Kerry came back with two from Ó Cinnéide. Armagh wouldn't lead again until the final score of the game.

In the meantime, it looked like Kerry were preparing to land the knockout blow. They were three points ahead when a goal-bound effort from Russell hit Kieran McGeeney's shoulder and went over the bar. Another chance fell to Eoin Brosnan, who was having the better of McGeeney, but the Kerry centre half-forward fired just wide. Cooper's second point put five between the teams with three minutes to half-time. Armagh got their chance when Oisin McConville collected a pass from Barry O'Hagan, on for a concussed McEntee, and headed for goal. Kerry goalkeeper Declan O'Keeffe stood in his way, but wrapped his legs around the Armagh forward to concede a penalty.

McConville stepped up to take the kick, knowing that in Armagh's 1953 and 1977 All-Ireland finals, they had missed penalties. History cruelly repeated itself when O'Keeffe saved McConville's kick. The Armagh support was still taking in this crushing *déjà vu* when Diarmaid Marsden scored with the last kick of the half to leave the score 0-11 to 0-7 in Kerry's favour.

Like the semi-final, Joe Kernan had something to show the Armagh players at half-time. However, he showed the wooden losers' plaque he had received in 1977 far less respect than the jersey he'd shown his players at the break against Dublin when he smashed it against the shower wall.

'Joe maybe thought we would be in a healthier position than we were at half-time,' says Tierney. 'He got emotional. He constantly told us we were a better team than in 1977 and he showed us what losing in an All-Ireland final got you.'

Kerry were out on the field for the second half long before Armagh, obviously having had less to talk about. If Russell and Liam Hassett had taken decent chances early in the restart, it's unlikely Armagh would have found a way back. Nevertheless, Tierney was still in no doubt as to the final outcome, even if many supporters weren't so sure.

'I know there were people in the crowd who thought we were going to be beat by fifteen points, and them Armagh people. You hear people say now, "I always knew they would win." But I know that the only people who thought Armagh were going to win were in that dressing room, and maybe family in the stands, but more in hope than anything else.'

Kerry were still four points up, 0-13 to 0-9 fifteen minutes into the half when Aidan O'Rourke set up Marsden for a goal chance that disappeared when the Kerry defence converged to give up a 'forty-five'. McConville pointed it, but Ó Cinnéide replied in kind ninety seconds later. It gave Kerry fourteen points to Armagh's ten. The Kingdom wouldn't score again.

Of course, nobody in Croke Park knew that, least of all Tierney. As he prepared to kick the ball out after Ó Cinnéide's point, Marsden decided to leave his corner-forward position under the Cusack Stand and make for the other side of the field.

'I was taking my run up and just remember thinking, "Where in the name of God is he going?" It definitely wasn't planned. He decided something needed to be done and did it.'

Marsden collected the ball and gave it to the overlapping wing-back Andy McCann, who transferred to McConville. His ball to Paul McGrane wasn't a good one, but McGrane managed to palm it back to McConville, who in turn fired low to the net. His penalty miss was instantly consigned to history.

'If you had seen Oisin McConville at half-time you wouldn't have thought he was going out,' says Tierney. 'That was character. He could have fisted a

After missing a penalty in the first half of the All-Ireland final, Oisin McConville was inconsolable. After scoring a goal in the second, redemption was written all over his face

point but he took the responsibility and turned the game for Armagh.'

McConville's goal left the northerners trailing by a point. O'Hagan had a chance to equalise with twelve minutes left, but his kick dropped well short and into the hands of Seamus Moynihan, who prepared to launch another Kerry attack. His kick went to midfield, but the only person there to collect was Kieran McGeeney. The Armagh captain seemed to have the field to himself. 'It looked like they had about eight men sent off,' remembers Tierney. McGeeney made the most of the space and picked out Clarke, who kicked the equaliser.

Darragh Ó Sé had a shot at goal in the sixty-second minute but it fell into

The Armagh support chair Kieran McGeeney from the field after the final whistle, while Kerry's Darragh Ó Sé gets caught up in the bedlam

Tierney's arms. Less than thirty seconds later Steven McDonnell kicked what proved to be the winner. The goalkeeper fills in the gaps:

'I remember catching the ball, looking up and seeing Bumpy (Barry O'Hagan) and Aidan O'Rourke out on the right, but they were both marked and I didn't want to hit a big high ball. I hit a pass, but I remember thinking, "One of you get a touch on it" because it was just a 50/50 ball. As it happened, Aidan touched it to Bumpy who gave it back to Aidan. It looked really cool, like something you had planned. Most people would have just looked for an easy hand-pass, but Aidan just hit the ball between three Kerry defenders to Stevie. It was exceptional.'

Ten more minutes passed until the final whistle, during which time Justin McNulty exorcised any ghosts of past Croke Parks with three vital interceptions, and Eoin Brosnan lined up a relatively simple shot at an equaliser. Tierney knew what was going to happen. At least he thought he did.

'I said a goalkeeper knows if it's over. Well, I was sure that was going to be a point. I remember thinking it was going over the middle of the bar, no doubt. I remember thinking I was going round to get the ball to kick out from the "twenty-one" and I saw the umpire was signalling a wide. I just laughed. It was our day.'

Kerry's final attack was broken up by Justin McNulty, whose interception fell to Tony McEntee, who gave the ball to McGeeney. With Armagh at 1-12 to Kerry's 0-14, John Bannon blew the final whistle, the Armagh fans invaded the pitch, and Tierney tried to take in what had just happened.

'I didn't cry, I didn't laugh. I just remember thinking, "Oh fuck, oh fuck, oh fuck, what have I done?" I wanted to get off as quickly as possible. I wouldn't be that fussed on crowds and I wanted to be beside McGeeney when he lifted the Cup. I could have stayed there all night. I wanted to talk to the crowd; I think I wanted the microphone off McGeeney at one stage. I felt like I was floating. It meant so much to us all. There's nothing like it in football. It's nice to be the best in Ireland at something.'

The best football team in Ireland in 2002 was:

ARMAGH 2002		
	Brendan Tierney	
Enda McNulty	**Justin McNulty**	**Francie Bellew**
Aidan O'Rourke	**Kieran McGeeney**	**Andrew McCann**
John Toal		**Paul McGrane**
Paddy McKeever	**John McEntee**	**Oisin McConville**
Steven McDonnell	**Ronan Clarke**	**Diarmaid Marsden**
Substitutes		
Barry O'Hagan for John McEntee; Tony McEntee for Paddy McKeever		

After a rendition of 'The Boys from the County Armagh' in the winners' changing room – 'The worst song in the world. I hate it,' says Tierney – the Armagh party moved on to the Citywest with Sam the guest of honour at the victory banquet.

'I went to bed about five, but hadn't that much to drink. I was up at eight o'clock the next morning and wanted up to see what was happening. The day after the final was the easiest I got out of bed in my life. My wife was pregnant at the time and didn't get much sleep, and at twenty-past eight we went down for breakfast and I said, "Not one of these fuckers will be up", but half the team was there. There was a party atmosphere in the breakfast room. Everybody was smiling. People weren't talking, they were just pointing at you and smiling.'

From Dublin, Armagh went through Meath and Louth to the county border near the Carrickdale hotel. It was here that Kieran McGeeney carried the Sam Maguire onto Armagh soil and where a huge reception committee of fans was gathered. Tierney was just a few miles from home. He remembered when he went to see Derry and Down bringing Sam north, never dreaming he would do it himself.

'I moved house, my wife had our daughter Aoife, I had the eleven-plus class at school and won the All-Ireland in the space of two months. I probably had more reasons for a nervous breakdown than anyone who ever went to a shrink, but it all worked out for the best. Every now and then, my son Conor would say, "Come on Daddy, let's watch Armagh", and I would put on the DVD and it still makes the hair stand up on the back of my neck.'

Another hair-raising moment, an encounter with his fellow Mullaghbawn man and captain Kieran McGeeney the day before the game, stands out for Tierney as one of his outstanding memories from the summer of 2002.

'In the Citywest the day before the match, Geezer, who I've grown up playing with at the club, pulled me aside, shook my hand and said, "All the best. After all your years of hard work and disappointment you're going to win an All-Ireland." Then he started laughing and I said, "Holy fuck, McGeeney. We're going to win this because you're laughing." It was a nice moment rather than a defining one, but it really stands out.

'The defining moment was probably when Joe Kernan rang me up and told me to make up my mind. There aren't many times in your life when all your decisions turn out for the best, but they did in 2002. Money couldn't buy what we had.'

Benny Tierney enjoys the moment with Sam

Kieran McGeeney with the ultimate prize

***Man of the Match:* Kieran McGeeney**
In the run-up to the 2002 All-Ireland final, Kieran McGeeney told journalists about the time when, not long after starting at Queen's University, he was sitting in Belfast's Botanic Inn declaring to those around him that he wanted to win an All-Ireland medal. The comment was greeted with derision in the bar. After all, Armagh had not won the Ulster title since 1982 and were not expected to be challenging for All-Ireland honour anytime soon. McGeeney didn't care. He knew what he wanted to do, and he knew there was no reason it couldn't happen.

That it did happen in 2002 was due in no small part to McGeeney, who inspired Armagh on a par with the best captains Gaelic football has known.

He already had a Sigerson Cup medal with Queen's and an Ulster Club championship with his native Mullaghbawn to his credit when he captured his first Ulster championship title with Armagh in 1999. He captained his county to the defence of that title the following year and lifted the Anglo-Celt again in 2002. His commanding presence, accurate distribution and generally inspirational play from centre half-back saw Armagh through games they might otherwise have lost.

In the All-Ireland final against Kerry he somehow managed to step up his performance level, dragging Armagh back into contention in the second half by almost completely taking over the game. One incident stands out: with twelve minutes left and Armagh a point down, McGeeney caught a clearance from the Kerry defence and, with not a soul near him, he kicked a perfect pass to Ronan Clarke to equalise. That's just the way Kieran McGeeney was in 2002 – nobody could touch him.

10

'Perfect'

TYRONE 2003

The following chapter is based on an interview with Cormac McAnallen that took place on Thursday, 22 January 2004. He had been troubled by a knee injury, and was working his way back to fitness. The Sunday after the interview, it was announced that the twenty-four-year-old would return to the Tyrone team as captain for the coming season. Having captained his county to All-Ireland wins at minor and under-21 levels, Cormac was the logical choice. Less than a month later he lifted his first senior trophy, the McKenna Cup.

Early on 1 March, Cormac died at his family home near Eglish of a viral infection of the heart. Three days later thousands of people came to the small Tyrone town to pay their respects at his funeral in St Patrick's Church.

I would like to take this opportunity to again thank Cormac's family for allowing me to publish this chapter as it was originally written, just two weeks after I had spoken to him. It is respectfully dedicated to his memory.

Baseball has 'The Catch' when Willie Mayes of the San Francisco Giants got to a seemingly ungettable ball in the 1954 World Series. Australian rugby union has 'The Tackle' when George Gregan stopped New Zealand's Jeff Wilson scoring the last minute try that would have won the Bledisloe Cup for the All Blacks in 1994. Tyrone football will always have 'The Block'.

Tyrone were leading their neighbours and fierce rivals Armagh by three points with four minutes remaining of the 2003 All-Ireland final, the first ever contested by two teams from the same province. Tyrone had held the lead from the fourth minute when Ger Cavlan scored to put them 0-2 to 0-1 ahead. They had also, however, missed a number of goal-scoring opportunities that would have put away the reigning champions. Just a goal behind, Armagh were still in the game and launched another attack on the opposition goal.

Steven McDonnell, the best goal-scorer in Ireland, who would be honoured as Footballer of the Year at the end of the season, received the ball inside the thirteen-metre line. As far as the formbook was concerned, the ball was in the net and the game was level, and such a swing in momentum would probably propel Armagh to victory. McDonnell dropped the ball and cocked his foot, ready to shoot past Tyrone goalkeeper John Devine. Conor Gormley was having none of it. The Carrickmore man hurled himself at the ball about to be dispatched to the net by McDonnell. At full stretch he cleanly stopped the ball and protected Tyrone's three-point lead – a lead they held until Brian White's whistle heralded a mass pitch invasion. At the game's end, Tyrone supporters followed in the footsteps of their Armagh counterparts the year before, totally ignoring the echoed requests to stay off the playing surface.

Like Armagh twelve months earlier – like Conor Gormley – they weren't going to be stopped when their moment came.

Tyrone supporters in Croke Park on 4 August 2002 must have wondered if they would ever see their county win an All-Ireland senior title. They had just watched their highly regarded side collapse against rank underdogs Sligo and crash out of the championship. The promise brought by spectacular underage success would go unfulfilled for another year. Teams with All-Ireland ambitions, they reasoned, shouldn't lose to Sligo; it was an embarrassment. Tyrone midfielder Cormac McAnallen disagreed.

'We were given an awful lot of stick for being beaten by Sligo, which I thought was unfair to us and insulting to Sligo because they were a good side. If we had played to our best against Sligo we would have beaten them, we just didn't take them out. We prepared well for the game and started very well, but at that stage I think we maybe started to believe what everybody had been telling us, that it would be an easy match, and we took our foot off the pedal. Sligo came back and never gave us a chance after that. While I was annoyed that we had been beaten by them I was in no way ashamed or anything like that. But a lot of people seemed to make us want to feel ashamed of it.'

The rest of the championship was just as uncomfortable for many Tyrone people, who could only watch as Armagh brought Sam back to Ulster. There were others, like McAnallen, who were delighted to see their neighbours achieve All-Ireland glory, and that win would provide inspiration for 2003.

'I was happy for them and I cheered them on in the final. I knew a lot of the fellas playing and I went to see their homecoming. It was great to see but, at the same time, I was very envious. You wondered: will it ever be us? What would it be like to be up there with the Cup?'

If McAnallen was ever to find out, it was going to be under new management. Mickey Harte took over as Tyrone senior manager from Art McRory and Eugene McKenna in November 2002. McAnallen, who had captained minor and under-21 teams to All-Ireland victories under Harte and his assistant Fr Gerard McAleer, always expected to work with him at senior level.

'It was probably going to happen sometime. It was always likely that when he wanted the job he would get it, but nobody really thought he would get it so quickly. Most people thought Art and Eugene would be there another year, but that's not the way it finished up.

'As players, we were sad to see things end the way they did for Art and Eugene as we had great respect for them and they had taken us to great things, with an Ulster title, and the county's first National League.

'Once the decision was made, we were happy to see Mickey there. He's a good man, and we'd had success with him before and we knew he would do well again.'

Harte secured his first senior silverware when Tyrone retained their National League title with a comfortable win over Laois, who had surprisingly beaten Armagh in the semi-final. It was a satisfactory way to start the season, but the real business started with Derry in the Ulster championship.

Tyrone and Derry's first round meeting was earmarked as the first 'big' game of the summer, but Monaghan stole the limelight a week before when they sent All-Ireland champions Armagh spinning out of the provincial championship. The free taking of Paul Finlay was crucial as he registered 0-8 to help Monaghan to a 0-13 to 0-9 win. It was a huge shock, but Armagh had been without Kieran McGeeney and Enda McNulty, while Oisin McConville was barely half-fit. There would be plenty of life left in Armagh's 2003.

Derry's championship that year got off to an inauspicious start when Tyrone took control of their first round match in Clones early in the first half. They scored the first four points of the match and dominated possession. However, for all their dominance, only Brian Dooher scored from play and they were dependent on Peter Canavan's accuracy from frees. Just before half-time, however, Canavan missed a simple one and Derry went in just four points down, 0-7 to 0-3, when they should have been out of it.

'We were very wary going in against Derry,' recalls McAnallen. 'We had done well in the league final, had played well, but we knew Derry would be sitting, getting together their plan, and we were ready to be chopped down.

'We had the wind advantage in the first half, we got a lead up, but we didn't really press it home, and we took it easy for a while. Derry came out in the second half and scored a goal and a couple of points early on which gave them the lead, with the wind, and from then on it was always going to be a dogfight. I personally thought we could have had the match won by half-time, but once there was only three or four points in it at half-time I knew it was going to go down to the wire.'

Derry were the only team in it for twenty-five minutes after the restart. The ten minutes after the break produced 1-4, the goal coming from Paddy Bradley. Conor Gormley was fortunate not to concede a penalty when his apparent pull on Dermot Dougan went unpunished. Ten minutes from the end Derry were four points up, 1-9 to 0-8, and the game seemed up for Tyrone, but four unanswered points, finished off with Canavan's sixth placed ball, earned them another shot.

Conor Gormley keeps Derry's Dermot Dougan at bay during the sides' Ulster championship replay

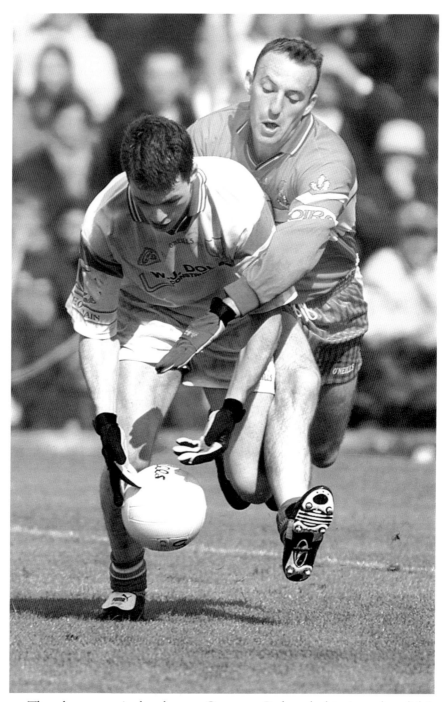

That shot came six days later at Casement Park and, this time, they didn't give Derry a chance. Their opponents could have been forgiven for having their minds elsewhere: in the early hours of Saturday morning Patricia Bateson, the twenty-year-old sister of Derry minor James, and a cousin of senior Kevin McGuckin, was killed in a road accident. The Tyrone v Derry minor replay, scheduled as a curtain-raiser to the senior game, was postponed, while McGuckin pulled out of the senior game.

On the field, Peter Canavan's free-taking proved decisive, the Tyrone captain scoring five in the first half. Young midfielder Sean Cavanagh also scored 0-3 from play in the first thirty-five minutes and Tyrone were 0-10 to 0-2 up at the break. The second half was a non-event as Tyrone kept the scoreboard ticking while Derry struggled to get into the game. Geoffrey McGonigle did manage a consolation goal, but it only kept the deficit down to single figures as Tyrone ran out 0-17 to 1-5 winners. McAnallen had only lasted ten minutes of the game before retiring with injury, but he liked what he saw from the sideline, even if it was obvious Derry weren't anywhere near the top of their game.

'Derry weren't themselves because of the death of Patricia Bateson. I can understand that some of the players were subdued. But we definitely played a whole lot better. We were a lot more organised, especially in defence. We supported each other better and got more breaking balls. We definitely upped our game and it was a matter of pride for us.'

By the time Tyrone returned to Casement for an Ulster semi-final clash with Antrim, Donegal's pride had taken a battering. Their first round defeat to Fermanagh, 0-10 to 0-6, was a comprehensive beating which manager Brian McEniff, who had stepped in when a replacement couldn't be found for Mickey Moran, described as one of the worst displays he had ever seen from a Donegal team. It was hard to argue, but like Armagh, Donegal were far from finished.

Eight points separated Tyrone and Antrim, but the final score, 1-17 to 1-9, didn't tell half the story. Tyrone dominated possession and managed to hit an astonishing twenty wides, but Antrim weren't put away until Owen Mulligan found the net in the sixty-eighth minute.

A Kevin Madden penalty after sixteen minutes gave Antrim a two-point lead, but Tyrone's makeshift midfield pairing of Ger Cavlan and Kevin Hughes enjoyed such superiority that McAnallen and Sean Cavanagh, both watching injured, were not missed. By half-time, Tyrone had eased into a four-point lead and continued their dominance after the interval, but profligate finishing meant Antrim were always in contention, although they couldn't get closer than four points. It's unlikely they would have narrowed the gap had the game gone on for another week, but McAnallen could never totally relax.

'I was worried with the chances we missed because the game was close for a long time and there were only three or four points in it until the goal. You can't be blasé about it. The game was there for the taking and if Antrim had got a goal the crowd would have got behind them and we would've been in trouble. I was worried about the number of wides, but the team played well as a unit and created a lot of chances, and played especially well going forward.'

RTE pundit Colm O'Rourke wasn't impressed with Tyrone's performance, but it was his criticism of one player in particular that grabbed

headlines. He told the *Sunday Game* audience the Tyrone team contained 'bad footballers', and singled out Brian Dooher. 'If Tyrone win an All-Ireland with Brian Dooher,' he said, 'I'll eat my hat.' Tyrone quietly resolved to shove O'Rourke's words down his throat as well.

The week before Tyrone booked their place in the Ulster final, Armagh and Donegal got their qualifier campaigns underway with wins over Waterford and Longford respectively. Oisin McConville and Steven McDonnell hit 2-11 between them as Armagh cantered to a 2-21 to 0-8 win, while eight Adrian Sweeney points helped Donegal to a 1-17 to 1-11 victory.

Armagh travelled to Casement Park for their second round qualifier and ground out a 0-15 to 0-12 win over Antrim, while Donegal enjoyed home advantage for their 0-16 to 0-11 triumph over Sligo. The week before the Ulster final both counties made their way to Croke Park for their third round qualifier games. Goals from Brendan Devenney and Brian Roper helped Donegal garner 2-19 to 0-15 over Tipperary in the opening attraction, while a superb second half display powered Armagh through at the expense of Dublin, 0-15 to 0-11.

Not many people outside Down thought their county had a chance against Tyrone in the Ulster final. Tyrone were being talked of as potential All-Ireland champions, while Down's first round win over Monaghan had been the county's first championship victory since 1999. Still, that most of the public and media was giving Down no chance was of little concern to Tyrone and a fit-again McAnallen.

'I can't say it really affected us that much because we knew what Down were capable of. They won their first two matches without playing well and I knew there was a big game in them. Nobody seemed to be playing all that brilliantly, but they won the games. If (Brendan) Coulter, (Liam) Doyle and those fellas clicked on one day you knew they could do damage. We thought the Ulster final might have been their day to turn it on, and so it was.'

In fact, the day belonged to both teams. The first half was unremarkable enough, distinguished by two fine saves from Down goalkeeper Mickey McVeigh. With half-time approaching, Tyrone enjoyed a 0-8 to 0-6 advantage, but Brendan Coulter put Down ahead with a brilliant individual goal in the first minute of injury time. There was still time left in the half for Gregory McCartan to be sent off for throwing the ball at Brian McGuigan after McGuigan had tripped him. Down managed to double their lead before the whistle but, with only fourteen men, it seemed unlikely to last long. It didn't – less than ten minutes into the second half they were nine up.

First Liam Doyle found the net, closely followed by Dan Gordon. Then Coulter finished off a brilliant move to leave three goals between the sides, 3-8 to 0-8. Tyrone were shell-shocked, but McAnallen didn't panic.

'It was a bit similar to the Derry match where we had a bit of an advantage in the first half, but we didn't press it home. We missed a few chances and, when Down got their chance, they punished us.

'It was a strange experience being nine points down and it took a fair bit of digging deep to come back from that. I don't want to appear cocky, but even when we were nine points down I felt there was a comeback in us – because there was enough time left. If that was the situation with ten minutes left, you would have been stupid to think you were going to come back, but with twenty-five minutes left I knew we had the capability to score. I knew we probably needed a goal somewhere along the line. I felt that if we got a point or two to get us started we would get on a roll. As it happened we got a goal, which was the best possible thing to happen. If we hadn't got that goal we might not have come back to get a draw.'

The goal came from a Peter Canavan penalty in the forty-eighth minute and that score sparked off a run of 1-6 without reply to level the scores after sixty-one minutes. Down might have crumbled, but Gordon found the net again and Tyrone were faced with another deficit to close. They managed it, Canavan's fifth free concluding the scoring and an astonishing game with Down 4-8, Tyrone 1-17. The replay was fixed for the following Sunday at Clones.

At training the Tuesday before the replay Mickey Harte took McAnallen aside and asked him how he would feel about playing full-back. Chris Lawn

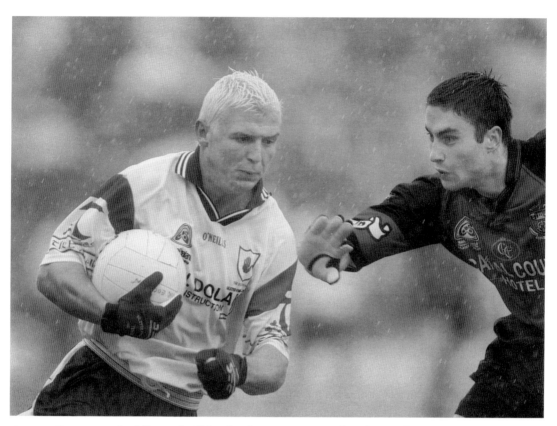

Owen Mulligan makes his way past Down's Adrian Scullion in the Ulster final replay

had limped off in the drawn game, and Colin Holmes still hadn't regained fitness, so Harte decided to bring his star midfielder back to the square. It could have been a daunting change of scenery, but McAnallen took it in his stride.

'You can't be fussy, especially at that time when a lot of players were coming back to fitness. You were just happy to be in the team. I was not long back from injury myself, so it wasn't as if I could afford to be fussy over where I was playing. With Mickey, if he picks you for somewhere, it's because he's thought about it and is confident in you to play there, so you go with it.'

As it turned out, the new full-back wasn't too busy during the replay.

'I remember standing at one end in the first half and being very nervous that the ball was going to come up, but we were winning most of the balls in midfield, and we won back most that we weren't when Down tried to play the ball away. We just put pressure on them throughout the field and, once there was a big enough gap built up, the game was really over.'

Clones was drenched by a massive shower just before the throw-in and the rain continued through the match. Tyrone steadily built up a comfortable lead, picking off points at will, and went in 0-11 to 0-3 at half-time. They didn't let up, and didn't allow Down any goal chances that might have sparked a revival. Peter Canavan finished with eleven points, mostly from frees, and Down had to wait until the third minute of injury time for Ronan Murtagh to find the net for a consolation goal. Even then, Tyrone had the

Sean Cavanagh was the find of the 2003 season. Here, he hand-passes away from danger during the All-Ireland quarter-final against Fermanagh

final say when Ger Cavlan earned the last point of the game to finish the scoring at 0-23 to 1-5.

While Tyrone were busy hammering Down, Armagh went about disposing of Limerick in their fourth round qualifier. Actually, Steven McDonnell disposed of Limerick as he contributed 3-4 in a 4-10 to 0-11 stroll. The night before, Fermanagh had continued their impressive run with a 0-12 to 1-8 win over beaten Connacht finalists Mayo. With Donegal waiting for the losers of the Ulster final replay, Armagh and Fermanagh's wins meant the province would have four teams in the All-Ireland quarter-finals.

Down had just six days to recover from the hiding Tyrone gave them, and they couldn't manage it, as Donegal registered an eight-point win in the fourth round of the All-Ireland qualifiers. Six points from Adrian Sweeney and goals from Christy Toye, Michael Hegarty and Stephen McDermott, helped Brian McEniff's side to a 3-15 to 2-10 win.

With the Ulster title taken, Tyrone eyes turned to their quarter-final draw. Roscommon, Donegal and Fermanagh were all possibilities, but the county was buzzing with the possibility of Armagh coming out of the hat. In the end

Fermanagh did. Armagh would have to wait, but Fermanagh weren't being taken lightly.

'The first thought was that it wasn't Armagh, as everybody in Tyrone was saying it was going to be. We were a bit wary of Fermanagh because we had beaten them in the National League and they would have felt they owed us one. Really, none of the four quarter-finalists were going to be easy. On that basis Fermanagh were the same as any other team. They knew us well; we knew them well.'

Tyrone also remembered what had happened twelve months earlier when Sligo made a mockery of them and their tag as pre-match favourites. It simply couldn't happen again.

'It was mentioned that Fermanagh could be our Sligo. That was mentioned to us the morning of the game, that if we didn't watch out it could be another Sligo. When we got into a good early lead that was an incentive to keep going and not take it easy.'

Tyrone were simply ruthless. They tore into Fermanagh and never let up until the final whistle heralded a crushing 1-21 to 0-5 victory. Ten different Tyrone players scored from play and only two of their twenty-two scores were from frees. The points went over in a constant stream from start to finish, while Sean Cavanagh provided the goal after sixteen minutes. Twelve points separated the teams at half-time, but it just got worse for Fermanagh, who could do little to stop Tyrone steamrollering them. For the second match in a row, Cormac McAnallen found little to test his full-back skills.

'On a day like that, when the team's going well you just enjoy it rather than wanting to get the game over. When you're that far ahead you can enjoy it, but before that it's a job of work.'

Pleased with a job well done, Tyrone personnel and fans could relax and take in the second quarter-final of the day, between Armagh and Laois. There was plenty to savour as both sides produced one of the best games of the year. Laois had been one of the stories of the summer, winning their first Leinster title since 1946, but Armagh proved too tough an obstacle to negotiate. Seven points from Oisin McConville were instrumental in helping the reigning champions through to a fiercely competed, hard-earned 0-15 to 0-13 win. It was impressive, and Tyrone knew it.

'I was impressed with the way Armagh ground it out,' says McAnallen. 'It looked at times that Laois might go into a winning run, but Armagh got it through winning the hard balls and being a little bit better organised. I was impressed with the way they toughed it out because Laois are a hard team to put away.'

Armagh's win meant they would face the winners of the next day's quarter-final between Donegal and Galway, while Tyrone would play Roscommon or Kerry. From that moment talk of an Armagh-Tyrone final dominated football discussion in Ulster, but it had been in the back of Tyrone minds a little earlier.

'We realised after the quarter-final draw was made that, if we won our quarter-final, we would play the winners of Kerry and Roscommon. We

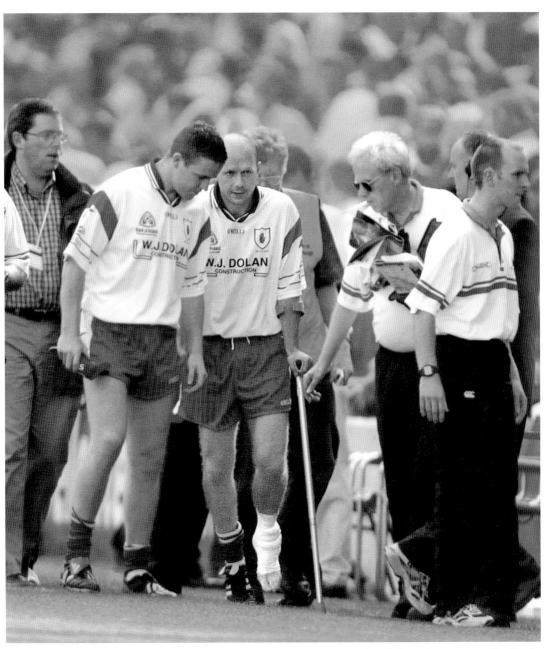

Peter Canavan's ankle injury, picked up early in the All-Ireland semi-final win over Kerry, was the talk of the county for the month before the final

didn't want to look too far ahead, but we realised that if we got to the final there was a good chance Armagh would be there.'

Armagh had to wait another week before they discovered their semi-final opponents. A late point from Kevin Walsh gave Galway a 1-11 to 0-14 draw with Donegal in Croke Park but, six days later in Castlebar, Donegal withstood a late Galway rally to record a 0-14 to 0-11 victory.

Ulster had produced three of the last four teams in the championship and was guaranteed a representative on All-Ireland final day. The Donegal-Armagh semi-final was the second down for deciding. First, Tyrone had the

Stephen O'Neill had the unenviable task of replacing Peter Canavan in the All-Ireland semi-final, but he played a vital role in helping Tyrone destroy Kerry

small matter of Kerry to deal with. Nobody anticipated the way the encounter panned out.

With two sets of potent forwards on display, an opening, high-scoring, exciting game was expected. As it turned out, Tyrone's defensive display took the laurels as they totally shut down the mighty Kingdom. Kerry managed just six points, only two in the first half, and just three from play. And Tyrone did it without Peter Canavan for an hour of the game.

Tyrone had scored the first three points when, in the twelfth minute, Canavan pulled out after tangling feet with Seamus Moynihan. The captain had damaged his ankle and was immediately replaced by Stephen O'Neill. The loss could have dealt Tyrone a fatal psychological blow, but it didn't work out that way.

'In a way it was good because it was at the start of the match,' says McAnallen. 'Everybody was so focused from the dressing room for the start that we were concentrating on playing our own game. Peter went off and we were straight into the game again. If it had been halfway through the second half it might have been more of a downer.

'At the time he went off we were so fired up to do our own thing that it didn't really affect our pattern of play. Maybe in the second half, when we were struggling to score, we could have used a man like Peter at that stage, but it didn't hold us back in the first half.'

It certainly didn't. Tyrone continued to crowd out the Kerry forwards and win the breaks around midfield. The Kerry players were given no space and, when Tyrone attacked, they took their chances, either from play or the frees the Kerry defence conceded as they soaked up constant pressure. By the time Colm Cooper opened Kerry's account in the twenty-fifth minute, Tyrone had already racked up six points. They added three more before the break, and went in 0-9 to 0-2 ahead, with one foot in the All-Ireland final. As the teams made for the changing rooms, Peter Canavan's daughter Aine took to the field to play in the primary schools' seven-a-side game. Meanwhile, under the Hogan Stand, Canavan, Cormac McAnallen and their team-mates were taking in what they had done in the previous thirty-five-plus minutes.

'It was probably our best half of football. It was a mixture of good attacking play and good defence. We could have had two or three goals and we held Kerry out well at the back. I'd be lying if I said there wasn't some surprise. We expected we were going to have to score an awful lot to beat Kerry because they had such good forwards. They were going to score most of their opportunities. So, for Kerry not to get too much ball and the ball they did get, they were under so much pressure they didn't score; and to only get two points, we were surprised. But, there was no way we could think about backing off or changing tactics. It had to be the foot down again.'

Kerry managed to come back into the game, but never found the goal they needed. Declan O'Sullivan blasted over with their best chance in the fiftieth minute and, while Tyrone were also finding it difficult to score, the advantage accrued in the first half always looked likely to see them through. Kerry crept to within four points, but scores from Stephen O'Neill, and two from the outstanding Brian Dooher, kept Tyrone ahead and helped them to a 0-13 to 0-6 tally at the final whistle, and into their third All-Ireland final.

On RTE's *Sunday Game* highlights programme that night Pat Spillane joined Colm O'Rourke in talking himself out of a Christmas card from Mickey Harte when he described the game as 'puke football'. The former Kerry legend objected to Tyrone's blanket defence, complaining that what he had witnessed wasn't the game he loved. Perhaps he loved Kerry winning too much. Cormac McAnallen certainly thought so.

'I think there was a bit of sour grapes in what he said. For us playing the game, we felt we had played a very good defensive game, and we did well to restrict them to six points and not let them get goals. If that's puke football, that's too bad. We go out to play attacking football, but there are times when you have to defend and when you do everyone is part of that.'

With Tyrone's victory, Sam was staying in Ulster, but his final destination was still unclear. Armagh and Donegal met in their semi-final a week after the first game and served up some exciting football, although the game was marked by Armagh's woeful shooting: they hit twenty wides.

Donegal took their fewer opportunities and, when Christy Toye finished off a brilliant move by hammering past Paul Hearty, Armagh's All-Ireland title was in serious jeopardy. The game swung back in Armagh's favour when Donegal full-back Raymond Sweeney was sent off early in the second half. A goal from Steven McDonnell, and Oisin McConville's injury-time penalty pulled them through to a 2-10 to 1-9 win.

A Tyrone-Armagh All-Ireland final was a nightmare for much of the rest of the country. Often accused of football parochialism, Ulster GAA experienced the other end of the wedge as many football folk in the other twenty-six counties adopted a semi-disinterested, almost scornful, approach to the big game. There seemed to be resentment that the northerners had gatecrashed the party and they would have little to contribute but negative, foul-ridden, dour football. Ulster took the resentment with the pinch of salt it deserved. Armagh and Tyrone couldn't care less, and the two counties went quite mad for four weeks.

McAnallen was perfectly placed to gauge the feeling in both counties. The former pupil at St Patrick's College in Armagh was prepared for the special attention he would get when he returned to his job teaching history and politics in St Catherine's Grammar School in the city.

'You would get comments passed every day walking down the corridor, in the staff room, walking down the street. Everywhere you went for those four or five weeks was crazy. I tried to enjoy it and roll with it for the first couple of weeks, but the last two weeks you really had to have a bit of time to yourself, and fill your head with your own thoughts and nobody else's.

'The time between the semi-final and the final really dragged. The days were long, especially when you were surrounded by people talking about it. It got tedious after a while, but we got through it okay.'

Most of Tyrone was wondering, hoping, praying, that Peter Canavan would get through the four weeks' build-up to the final all right and lead the team out on 28 September. The uncertainty wasn't confined to the supporters.

'I didn't really ask too many questions and, whenever I did, nobody was really too sure. The decision was only taken a day or two before the match. The team wasn't sure, Peter was unsure, Mickey was unsure. We just had to get on with it, regardless of whether Peter would start or not.'

The Friday before the game Mickey Harte made the decision to start Canavan, hope his damaged ankle could withstand twenty-five or thirty minutes, take him off, and re-introduce him for the last ten or fifteen minutes.

'It wasn't really made known to the players. Mickey was probably doing that because the game was about fifteen players, not just about Peter. The players had enough to worry about on their own without worrying too much about Peter. Mickey's attitude would be that if the fifteen players weren't good enough to win it, we wouldn't win it with Peter. Mickey had his plan, but I can't say I knew, and can't say I cared too much – as long as we were ahead on the scoreboard.'

Tyrone were in front, as it turned out, for all but three minutes of the final. John McEntee's point cancelled out Peter Canavan's opener, but was itself quickly followed by a Ger Cavlan score. Tyrone would never lose the lead Cavlan's point gave them. As anticipated, the hits were thundering in from both sides, but Tyrone used their possession better and got the ball into positions where Armagh's illegal hits yielded scoreable frees. Canavan added two more, while Brian McGuigan and Steven McDonnell shared points to see Tyrone 0-5 to 0-2 ahead approaching the twentieth minute.

Then, the first of Tyrone's four clear chances at the net fell to Sean Cavanagh. Owen Mulligan and Enda McGinley combined to find Brian McGuigan, whose advance on goal was halted by Paul McGrane. McGuigan managed to get the ball to Cavanagh but, under pressure from onrushing Armagh keeper Paul Hearty, the midfielder screwed his shot wide.

Canavan and Oisin McConville swapped frees before McDonnell shaved Armagh's deficit to two with a superb point in the twenty-eighth minute. Canavan added another free shortly after, but it was clear that his ankle was giving him serious problems. Brian McGuigan was having problems too. A stomach bug picked up earlier in the week had taken its toll on the centre half-forward and Stephen O'Neill replaced him. Mickey Harte was hatching another plan.

Back on the Tyrone square, Cormac McAnallen had his hands full with Steven McDonnell. Before the game, many in the media thought Ryan McMenamin would pick up the brilliant McDonnell rather than McAnallen, who was still learning how to play the position at the highest level.

'At midfield you can follow the ball, go wherever you like and try to dictate the game. You don't have as much control over the game; you can only deal with whatever people give you. That's something you get used to, but when you're playing your fourth game in the position and it's the All-Ireland final, it's hard to get your head around at times. You feel like you need a bit more practice and, with Steven McDonnell around, it's hard enough if you've played there all your life.'

Tyrone fashioned, and squandered, another goal chance in injury-time. O'Neill fed Cavanagh, who played in to Enda McGinley with only Hearty to beat. He hit the target, but Hearty got his leg to the ball and deflected it over for Tyrone's eighth point. They went in at the break leading by four points.

When Tyrone returned to the pitch they were without Canavan, who was receiving treatment in the changing room for his ankle. A revitalised Brian McGuigan, returning after a fluid top-up for the second half, took his place.

Five minutes in, Stephen O'Neill gave Ger Cavlan the chance to bury Armagh but he pulled his low shot wide. The next four scores came from frees as the game became increasingly scrappy. Paddy McKeever and Mulligan hit two each to push Tyrone 0-10 to 0-7 ahead with just over twenty minutes left.

Another Armagh attack was frustrated in the fifty-fifth minute and Tyrone prepared to take a relieving free-out. Away from the main action Philip

Kevin Hughes was everywhere for the seventy minutes of the All-Ireland final and picked up man of the match honours at the end of it. Paul McGrane witnesses some of the Tyrone man's fancy footwork here

Jordan made for Diarmaid Marsden, who sent Jordan to the turf. Jordan was booked for his charge at Marsden, and the latter was sent off by Brian White. Armagh weren't deterred and continued to attack, but solid Tyrone defence, and some wasted possession kept them adrift. A McConville free pulled them to within two, but O'Neill then restored Tyrone's three-point advantage with an excellent score. Two minutes later Mulligan somehow managed to blaze against the post when presented with a gift of a chance to wrap up the match. It was Tyrone's fourth clear miss when in on goal. Cormac McAnallen was more than a little anxious.

'It wasn't the sort of game where your nerves went away and you relaxed. It was such a tight game and I was very aware of the importance of every ball

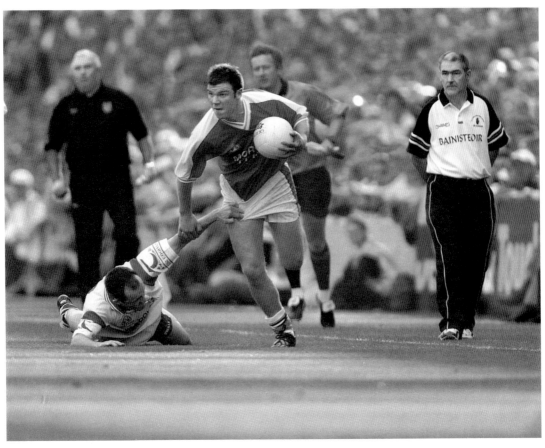

Tyrone manager Mickey Harte and his Armagh counterpart Joe Kernan watch as Ronan Clarke shakes off Brian Dooher

I went for. Coming down the stretch you were aware that, with a two-point lead, one slip or one moment from Armagh could turn the game. When Stephen O'Neill scored the last point, I thought, time was nearly up; we're three points ahead, maybe that's it. But still, Armagh could win the next ball, pump it into our square and anything could happen.'

Two minutes from the end of normal time, 'The Block' happened. McAnallen remembers it well, despite not seeing it.

'A high ball came in and I called for it. I thought Sean Cavanagh was staying down, but he jumped with me. Both of us nearly got our hands to it and it bounced off both of us, we bounced off each other, and the ball fell to Tony McEntee. Once he got the ball, I was on my knees and I tried to dive to pull the ball back or get a touch on his hand, but he got his fist-pass to McDonnell who was lying in behind. When he got the ball I thought, "Goal here" because he was six yards out and, although John Devine was coming out, McDonnell's such a good finisher. I just thought, "He's putting that away."

'I didn't see Conor Gormley at all. I didn't even see the block. I might have had my face in the ground thinking the ball was in the net. It was unbelievable. A lifesaver, and that's it.'

Armagh managed to win a free from the ensuing play, which McConville

*Peter Canavan
finally gets his hands
on Sam Maguire*

pointed to bring the deficit to two points. Three minutes of injury time was announced and, halfway through, O'Neill finished off a five-man move to clinch Tyrone's first All-Ireland final victory 0-12 to 0-9. A little over ninety seconds later Brian White blew the final whistle. The ball was in the hands of 'bad footballer', and now All-Ireland champion, Brian Dooher. Croke Park exploded. Cormac McAnallen didn't know what to do.

'I had to take a wee look around to make sure there was a whistle, that everybody had heard a whistle, and the game was over. Once I was sure of that I just lost myself.'

So did the Tyrone supporters who flooded onto the field. The players who didn't beat the surge were carried shoulder-high to the Hogan Stand to see Peter Canavan lift the Sam Maguire and strike his name from the top of the list of 'best players never to have won the All-Ireland'. Then Canavan delivered a speech that encapsulated just about everything this All-Ireland victory meant. In it he paid tribute to the players, management, backroom staff and fans, to former players who didn't quite achieve what the squad of 2003 just had, and to Art McRory and Eugene McKenna. He also spoke of his father Sean, who had passed away the week before the Ulster final, and of Paul McGirr.

On 15 June 1997, ten minutes into their first round game against Armagh in the Ulster minor championship, Tyrone's left half-forward Paul McGirr dived for a ball in front of the Armagh goal and fisted it to the net. In scoring, the eighteen-year-old from Dromore collided with the goalkeeper and didn't get up. He was stretchered off the field and taken to Tyrone County Hospital with suspected broken ribs.

In fact, the collision had torn the main artery away from his liver and after massive blood loss McGirr suffered cardiac arrest and died. Mickey Harte and Fr Gerard McAleer were the managers of the Tyrone minors at the time. The team went on to lose the All-Ireland final that year to Laois.

Twelve months later Cormac McAnallen was captain when Tyrone beat Laois in the final. Over the 2000 and 2001 seasons McAnallen led many of McGirr's minor team-mates to successive All-Ireland under-21 titles. Now those same players, who had since progressed into the ranks of their county's senior squad, watched as their captain, Peter Canavan, became the first Tyrone man to lift the Sam Maguire. For McAnallen, Declan McCrossan, Ciaran Gourley, Brian McGuigan, Kevin Hughes, Mark Harte and Stephen O'Neill – the man who had replaced McGirr on that tragic day six years previously – Canavan's tribute to their deceased friend was an emotional moment.

'It was perfect,' recalls McAnallen. 'Peter is the man you want to be lifting Sam. You're not that high up in the presentation box, so it's hard to get an idea of how many people were there. It's only when you see the shots from high up in the stand that you realise how many people were actually there.'

For the thousands on the field, and the Tyrone players, it was simply a dream come true.

'You were in a wee bit of disbelief at that stage. It's something you picture yourself doing so much and you had seen it in your own mind, walking up the steps and lifting Sam. It was like you had imagined. The dressing room was something special. About half an hour after the match it all went quiet and everybody just took a wee minute to take it all in. We were waiting about for a while for a few fellas coming back from drug tests, but nobody cared.'

Tyrone's history makers on 28 September 2003 were:

TYRONE 2003

John Devine

Ciaran Gourley   Cormac McAnallen   Ryan McMenamin

Conor Gormley   Gavin Devlin   Philip Jordan

Sean Cavanagh   Kevin Hughes

Brian Dooher   Brian McGuigan   Ger Cavlan

Enda McGinley   Peter Canavan   Owen Mulligan

Substitutes

Stephen O'Neill for Brian McGuigan; Brian McGuigan for Peter Canavan; Colin Holmes for Ciaran Gourley; Peter Canavan for Ger Cavlan; Chris Lawn for Conor Gormley

Waking up the next day as All-Ireland champions meant doing so with a few sore heads and stepping into a wave of euphoria that would engulf Tyrone, and Tyrone people everywhere, for months to come.

'You didn't have a minute to yourself because the moment you woke up you were trying to get breakfast, and there was a crowd in the lobby. Trying to get your bags on to the bus, little things like that were impossible; you were being mobbed. If you thought you could unwind the morning after, you had another thing coming.

'The homecoming, especially Omagh, was amazing. I don't think it has ever been beaten before for a homecoming and it'll take a lot of beating by any team.'

While other Tyrone players took time off work to celebrate their victory, McAnallen, who was set to tour Australia with the Irish International Rules team, knew he needed to get back to school to put some hours in before he took more time off. The Thursday after the final he returned to work in the heart of Armagh.

'There wasn't a whole lot said. I didn't say a lot either. I think I just had a big cheesey grin on my face. I didn't rub it in. They knew.'

Man of the Match: Peter Canavan

Like almost all of Tyrone's All-Ireland winning team, Peter Canavan's footballing curriculum vitae is adorned with underage success.

He played a starring role as captain of the Tyrone teams that won All-Ireland under-21 titles in 1991 and 1992. In 1995 he came as close as anyone before or since to winning an All-Ireland final on his own. Having inspired his county to their first Ulster title in nine years, then a semi-final win over Galway, he scored 0-11 of their 0-12 total in the final against Dublin. The

Dubs were leading by a point, 1-10 to 0-12, when Canavan made his most telling contribution, flicking the ball to Sean McLaughlin, who sent over the equaliser. Unfortunately for Tyrone, referee Paddy Russell judged Canavan had touched the ball on the ground and the score was disallowed. Sam left Ulster for the first time in four years and wouldn't return for another seven.

In the meantime Canavan continued to produce virtuoso displays, captaining Tyrone to their 2001 and 2002 National League titles. In 2003 he led the charge for the county's first All-Ireland. A vital penalty changed the course of the Ulster final when it seemed Down were set for victory. The ankle injury he picked up early in the All-Ireland semi-final preoccupied the entire county as the final against Armagh loomed. When the big day came around he led his team out and helped them into a half-time lead before retiring at the break to have his ankle attended to. He returned ten minutes from the end to help Tyrone over the finish line.

Even GAA president Sean Kelly was impressed, telling the crowd, on handing Sam over to Canavan, what an honour it was to present the famous trophy to 'Peter the Great'.

Peter Canavan

Epilogue

Antrim's Colin Brady gets to grips with Donegal's Brendan Devenney as fellow Saffron Niall Ward closes in during the sides' Ulster championship contest in Ballybofey

The Sam Maguire didn't come north in 2004. Instead, it travelled the well-worn route to Kerry to spend yet another winter in the Kingdom.

For much of the year it seemed that Sam would be staying in Ulster. Armagh emphatically showed how much they wanted their title back with an Ulster final demolition of Donegal; and Tyrone's determination to keep their crown was illustrated by their impressive win over Galway. Later in the season two of the province's most unusual suspects, Fermanagh and Derry, suggested

Ulster might have a summer of glory no one could have predicted.

In the end the glory went elsewhere, and while this book did not set out to chronicle the disappointments Ulster teams have suffered, 2004 provides a fitting epilogue to what has gone before. The season brought another historic all-Ulster occasion at Croke Park, one of the biggest upsets in living memory, and the cruel loss of one of the GAA's brightest stars.

 Normal service was resumed in Ulster during the first two months of 2004. An expanded McKenna Cup competition was won by Tyrone, with Cormac McAnallen lifting the trophy after a comprehensive final win over Donegal in Ballybofey.

There was more success for Ulster at the end of February when a Sligo Institute of Technology side, packed with Donegal players, beat a Queen's University team, managed by Down legend James McCartan, in the Belfast final of the Sigerson Cup. McAnallen, who had picked up a Sigerson medal with Queen's in 2000, was at the game. Three days later the news of his death was a stunning shock for the GAA and much of the rest of the country. Tributes poured in for days, as did sympathy for his parents Brendan and Brigid, brothers Fergus and Donal, and fiancée Ashleen.

The Tyrone panel and management, many of whom had dealt personally with the death of McAnallen's minor team-mate Paul McGirr in 1997, now had another tragedy to absorb. They returned to the field of play against Mayo in a National Football League game in Castlebar. Conor Gormley, the newly-installed full-back, wore the number 31 jersey, as he would throughout the season. McAnallen's number 3 shirt was laid to rest, and every Tyrone team-sheet served as a reminder of his loss.

Mickey Harte's men surrendered their league title after an epic, two-game semi-final tie with Galway who, in turn, lost the league final to Kerry. The following week Tyrone began the defence of their Ulster and All-Ireland titles, well aware of the 'hoodoo' that stalks teams drawn in the preliminary round of the provincial championship. Twelve months earlier the then All-Ireland champions Armagh had fallen at the same hurdle against Monaghan, but Derry never looked like repeating the feat as Tyrone pulled away and crossed the line with plenty to spare, 1-17 to 1-6.

The reaction in Tyrone was general satisfaction at a job well done, while in Derry, supporters and former players let rip against their county's display. 1993 All-Ireland winner Damian Barton began his column in the following day's *Irish News* with a concise summation of the team's performance: 'Gutless, spineless, toothless, humiliating and embarrassing.' Another Derry great, Joe Brolly, called for manager Mickey Moran's resignation, a call echoed by Donegal legend Martin McHugh. Moran listened, but defended his position stoutly and went about preparing his charges for their next game – a qualifier clash in Aughrim against Wickow, who had beaten them in the National League.

While Derry tried to pick themselves up, their old manager led his new county into championship battle. Eamonn Coleman's Cavan appeared to

have sealed victory against Down in Casement Park when the Mourne side's John Clarke stole a late point to level scores at 1-13 apiece. Two weeks later, in the replay at Breffni Park, Down seemed to be in control, but the introduction of former All-Star Dermot McCabe inspired the home side to a four-point win, 3-13 to 2-12. Cavan's victory earned them a semi-final clash with Armagh, who had exorcised all ghosts of twelve months before when they thrashed Monaghan 2-19 to 0-10.

On the same day as the Cavan v Down replay, Donegal spluttered to a 1-15 to 1-9 win over Antrim at MacCumhaill Park in Ballybofey. The men from the hills awaited the winners of Tyrone's clash with Fermanagh, but most people considered that game a mere formality, with Tyrone expected to repeat the hammering they gave the Ernemen in the 2003 All-Ireland quarter-final. Since then Fermanagh's manager, Dominic Corrigan, had been replaced by Donegal man, Charlie Mulgrew. A number of experienced players, including young forward Ryan Keenan, had departed due to a variety of reasons. In the run-up to the Tyrone game, Keenan claimed in the *Irish News* that the Mulgrew approach wasn't working. Referring to the players who had accompanied him off the panel, Keenan said, 'I think a lot of the boys realised that we weren't going to do a lot this year.'

Mulgrew kept his counsel on the whole affair and named five debutants for the Tyrone match. The bookies didn't give Fermanagh a chance, picking Tyrone as almost unbackable favourites. As usual, the bookies were right: Tyrone won, but only by four points; and while the All-Ireland champions left Clones relieved, Fermanagh left the grounds with an enormous amount of pride restored.

That was all very well, but they still had only six days to prepare for the long journey to Thurles and a qualifier meeting with Tipperary. The county board was considering appealing to the Games Administration Committee of the GAA to get the match put back a week when fate intervened to give Fermanagh's summer a nudge in the right direction. The mid-Tipperary board fixed a championship hurling match for the Wednesday before the game with Fermanagh. This would have resulted in two members of Andy Shortall's squad playing just three days in advance of facing Fermanagh. Shortall resigned and, in an act of solidarity, the Tipperary players said they wouldn't play against Fermanagh. With no team to field, the Tipperary board informed the GAA they wouldn't be fulfilling the fixture and Fermanagh got a bye to the next round of the qualifiers.

On the day after Fermanagh had been due to play Tipp – which was also the day Derry finished, having five points to spare against Wickow – Armagh lined up against Cavan in the Ulster semi-final. The expectation was that Armagh would safely negotiate the hurdle and, barely a minute after the whistle, with Cavan's Pearse McKenna already sent off, there was no reason to believe anything would change. Cavan stuck at it, however, with Mark McKeever leading the charge, and were three points up, 0-9 to 0-6, thirteen

Tyrone's Sean Cavanagh surrounded by jubilant Mayo supporters after the All-Ireland quarter-final

minutes into the second half. Armagh rallied and were level with thirteen more minutes left on the clock, but Breffni's finest didn't give up and continued to push forward despite being a man down. As the game entered injury time, Cavan led 0-11 to 0-10, but Oisin McConville's equaliser knocked the wind out of Coleman's side, and points from Diarmaid Marsden and Brian Mallon finally put them away. It was difficult to miss the collective sigh of relief from the Armagh players, management and supporters.

There had been plenty of talk in the media that, with Ulster football at a high watermark, the only place capable of hosting a meeting between Armagh and Tyrone was Croke Park. The week before the Fermanagh v Tyrone match, Ulster council president Michael Greenan refuted newspaper reports that the provincial final would take place in Dublin if it proved to be a repeat of 2003's All-Ireland final. Greenan stated that the venue had not yet been decided. Nevertheless, in the week before Tyrone's semi-final against Donegal, the Ulster council publicly announced the final would be in Croke Park, whatever the outcome of the following Sunday's game.

The Ulster semi-final began in terrible conditions at Clones. Tyrone got to grips with the rain, greasy ball and slippery conditions quicker than their opponents, bagging the first two points of the match. However, approaching half-time, they were just a point ahead, 0-3 to 0-2, as both sides sets of forwards increasingly found the conditions too much for them. It was then that Niall McCready tangled with Owen Mulligan and received his second yellow card. The teams swapped points before the interval, but things were looking grim for the fourteen-man Donegal side.

The Derry team celebrate their quarter-final win over Leinster champions Westmeath

Fermanagh fans show their colours as they cheer their county on against Mayo

Whatever was said in the Donegal changing room at half-time clearly worked because there was only one team in it after the break. Under captain Adrian Sweeney's leadership, and with Colm McFadden rampant up front, Donegal tore into Tyrone and achieved a win that was much more comfortable than the resulting 1-11 to 1-9 margin suggests.

As Donegal and Armagh prepared for the provincial final, the remaining northern teams in the championship readied themselves for the qualifiers, which featured two all-Ulster ties: Down against Tyrone, and Cavan against Derry. The Cavan v Derry game attracted the most attention as it pitted Eamonn Coleman against Mickey Moran, who had been the trainer of Derry's 1993 All-Ireland winning team.

The game at Celtic Park was one of the strangest of the summer. Derry controlled it for the most part, but Cavan stayed in it with a couple of goals, and Derry eventually needed a late point from full-back Niall McCusker to force extra time. It was 0-15 to 2-9 when the additional period of play started, but Derry reeled off ten points without reply to leave both Coleman and Cavan stunned.

Extra time was also required in Enniskillen on the previous evening when Fermanagh squeezed past Meath, 0-19 to 2-12. There was less drama in Newry as Tyrone got back on track with a fairly sedate 1-15 to 0-10 win over Down. The draw for the next round of the qualifiers woke Tyrone up, though, as they were pitted against Galway, a match fixed for a Croke Park double-header with Fermanagh's game with Cork. All of that would have to wait, however, until the next game scheduled for Croke Park was out of the way. And that next game was something really out of the ordinary.

Clones was the proverbial ghost town on 11 July when Donegal, Armagh and the minors of Tyrone and Down headed to Dublin, bringing their provincial deciders with them. The Ulster final had been played at Croke Park before – in 1939 – when Armagh's meeting with Cavan was relocated to GAA headquarters after the first game at Castleblayney was abandoned due to repeated pitch incursions by the large crowd.

Croke Park had no problem dealing with the record 67,136 attendance that filed through the turnstiles, expecting a tight, exciting game between two evenly-matched sides. Instead, the crowd witnessed a footballing bloodbath.

Armagh nabbed the first four points and, while Donegal pulled to within one, Joe Kernan's men never gave up the lead, and never really looked like doing so. Their first goal came when Diarmaid Marsden flicked in an Oisin McConville 'forty-five' after twenty-eight minutes. The second half was a procession as Armagh picked off points at will and Donegal struggled to get

The dark clouds gather over Fermanagh manager Charlie Mulgrew as he sees his side's All-Ireland dream slip away in the last minutes of their semi-final replay against Mayo

Team selector Sylvester Mulrone and Martin McGrath show their disappointment after Fermanagh's defeat at the hands of Mayo

near them. Goals from Paddy McKeever and McConville completed the most impressive team performance of the entire championship, and Kieran McGeeney lifted the Anglo-Celt for the third time against the unfamiliar backdrop of the Hogan Stand.

The following week, Fermanagh and Tyrone made the trip to Croke Park, and both were expected to find it tough against Cork and Galway respectively. Fermanagh were aiming for their first ever senior championship win at the venue, but memories of past Croke Park disappointments started to stir ten minutes into the second half when Cork opened up a three-point lead, 0-10 to 0-7. In a situation when previous Fermanagh teams had folded, the 2004 vintage found an extra gear, reeling off five unanswered points to push into a 0-12 to 0-10 lead. Cork got the next one, but Fermanagh weren't going to be denied and outscored Cork by a further six points to one as they cantered across the line. It was a blistering display.

All Ulster eyes then turned to Tyrone and, for most of their clash with Galway, it looked like it would be the tight encounter most anticipated. A Brian McGuigan goal twelve minutes in gave Tyrone a one-point lead, but Galway missed chances – most glaringly a penalty by Derek Savage. Two points separated the sides at the break, and Tyrone led by three when Peter Canavan, out of action since the previous year's All-Ireland final, made his return to action. Canavan's introduction lifted his county and they gradually took control, moving beyond Galway's reach and reasserting their All-Ireland credentials with a 1-16 to 0-11 win.

Tyrone were even more impressive in their next qualifier outing, basically wrapping things up by half-time against Laois and finishing 3-15 to 2-4 ahead. Derry's improbable run continued with a 0-10 to 0-7 win over Limerick, while Fermanagh needed extra time to end Donegal's championship interest, 1-10 to 0-12.

With five teams in the All-Ireland quarter-finals Ulster football could be justifiably pleased with itself, although Fermanagh followers winced when they were pulled out of the hat next to Armagh. Not one pundit gave the Erne players a chance and many predicted a repeat of the hammering they received from Tyrone at the same stage the year before. That looked like a frightening likelihood early on as Armagh clipped over the first four points, picking the Fermanagh defence apart. Crucially, Fermanagh kept their goal

Derry's Enda Muldoon fights his way past Kerry's Michael McCarthy in the counties' All-Ireland semi-final meeting

intact and started to dictate things, moving into a 0-8 to 0-6 lead at half-time. They also enjoyed a personnel advantage going into the second thirty-five minutes after Enda McNulty was sent off for unnecessarily following through with his forearm and connecting with Marty McGrath's chin.

Armagh weren't done and led 0-9 to 0-8 when captain Kieran McGeeney pointed. The sides continued to swap points, but Fermanagh missed as many as they scored, and Oisin McConville gave Armagh an 0-11 to 0-10 gain which was lost when Tom Brewster levelled. Eleven minutes passed without a score before Brewster appeared again to stroke over the most famous point in Fermanagh's football history.

The pitch was still heavy with jubilant Fermanagh supporters when Tyrone and Mayo took to the field for their quarter-final. Mayo jumped into an early lead, but Tyrone stayed with them while never playing particularly well. Ger Cavlan hit the final point of the half to leave the All-Ireland champions trailing 0-9 to 0-7 at the break. Ten minutes into the second half Mayo were leading 0-12 to 0-9, but Stephen O'Neill hammered Tyrone level with a brilliant goal. They didn't score again. With Kieran McDonald pulling the strings, Mayo ended Tyrone's reign at the top with four more points. As the Mayo fans replicated Fermanagh's post-match pitch invasion, Tyrone's players, management and supporters reflected on the end of a remarkable, emotional season.

A scheduling quirk meant Derry, yet to play their quarter-final against Westmeath, were still in the championship while Tyrone were out, something few people would have predicted after the teams' May meeting in Clones. Derry weren't fancied to go a round further than Tyrone, but goals from Paddy Bradley and Enda Muldoon had them 2-5 to 0-7 ahead at half-time. Westmeath, wearing the mantle of Leinster champions for the first time, steadily moved back into the game, finally edging ahead with ten minutes left, and looking the more likely to make the last four. Substitute Eamon Burke hit over an excellent score to level things; then Enda Muldoon took over. First the Ballinderry man hit over a brilliant go-ahead point; then he kept his cool to arrow over the clincher from a difficult free. An all-Ulster All-Ireland final was still on, but not the one anybody had imagined.

It was still on as the last weekend in August approached: Derry were to face Kerry on the Sunday, the day after Fermanagh and Mayo replayed their semi-final. The replay came when, on the first day, the sides played out a 0-9 to 0-9 draw in terrible conditions. As the teams' second encounter loomed closer, there was no escaping the feeling that Fermanagh had lost their chance.

The first outing saw Mayo lead 0-6 to 0-5 at half-time after Fermanagh had scored the game's first three points. Charlie Mulgrew's side were guilty of wasting a number of good chances, a habit that continued into the second half, even after Mayo's James Gill had been sent off. They needed a late Stephen Maguire free to level scores at 0-9 each, but still found time to miss a couple of match-winning opportunities. Mayo boss John Maughan – a former Fermanagh manager – was aware that his side had dodged a bullet, and they made the most of their second chance six days later when they held their nerve to produce a late scoring burst that sealed a 0-13 to 1-8 win.

Fermanagh started the replay poorly, but stayed in the game thanks to a James Sherry goal five minutes before half-time. Without it they would have been gone by the break and they took heart from the score, starting the second half with three points to push ahead 1-6 to 0-8. Scores seesawed until Mayo found the reserve to grab the last three points of the game and finally run Fermanagh's fairytale bandwagon off the road.

The following day Derry carried Ulster championship hopes out against Kerry and, for almost half-an-hour, the Northerners went toe-to-toe with the Kingdom, thanks mainly to a goal from Enda Muldoon. From the twenty-sixth minute, however, Kerry dominated and Declan O'Sullivan's second half goal capped a period during which they outscored Derry 1-13 to 0-2. With the game won Kerry took their foot off the pedal, allowing Derry to take the last five scores of the game. At the finish, the board read 1-17 to 1-11. There was never any chance the Munster men would be beaten, never any chance 2004 would be Ulster's season.

Still, there would always be next year…